Top 100 Trump

Promises Made Promises Kept

Ed Martin
with Jordan Henry

Permission to quote in critical reviews with citation:

Top 100 Trump Promises Made Promises Kept
by Ed Martin

Print ISBN 978-1-949718-07-2

Skellig
AMERICA

TABLE OF CONTENTS

34. Get Out Of TPP
35. Get Rid Of The Marriage Penalty
36. Give Dr. Ben Carson A Place In His Administration
37. Give Economic Prosperity To Hispanic Communities
38. Give The Facts Plainly And Honestly—Keep Tweeting!
39. Grow The American Economy
40. Hire Americans First
41. Honor Hero Dog Conan At The White House
42. If Manufacturers Leave There Will Be Consequences
43. Increase Government Transparency
44. Increase Oil Production
45. Keep Ford In The United States
46. Keep Gitmo Open
47. Limit Legal Immigration
48. Lots More ICE Agents
49. Lower Repatriation Tax For Businesses
50. Make A Vote For Trump The Best You Ever Cast
51. Work With The State Of Israel
52. Make Healthcare Prices More Transparent
53. Make Japan Pay Its Fair Share For Military Protection
54. Make Our Country Rich Again
55. Make Our NATO Allies Pay Their Fair Share
56. Make The "Brand" Of America Great Again
57. Move U.S. Embassy To Jerusalem
58. Neutralize Defense Sequestration
59. Never Be In A Bicycle Race
60. Never Ever Stop Fighting
61. Nobody Will Be Pushing Us Around
62. Nominate Pro-Life Justices
63. Not Be Controlled By Lobbyists
64. Only Let In Immigrants Who Love Americans
65. Pick Judges Who Support Second Amendment
66. Pick Judges Who Uphold the Constitution
67. Pick Someone From His List To Replace Justice Scalia
68. Place Lifetime Ban On White House Officials Lobbying For Foreign Governments
69. The Powerful Won't Beat Up On People Who Cannot Defend Themselves
70. Prioritize Mental Health Care
71. Protect All Kids Equally
72. Protect American Intellectual Property
73. Protect Religious Freedom
74. Pull Out Of Iran Deal
75. Put Americans First

Dedication

To the American people who know
that putting America First means
getting our house in order:
God, Family, Nation.

And to the men and women
who serve in our Armed Forces
and law enforcement:
thank you for protecting us.

Introduction

"He Made Promises. He Kept His Promises."

Donald Trump filled the doorway as Phyllis Schlafly and I looked up from our plastic seats. We needed one more chair in this tiny dressing room where I imagine showgirls did makeup and set their costumes. We were just a few feet off the stage of the Peabody Opera House in downtown St. Louis: me, Phyllis Schlafly and the next President of the United States of America.

It was early March 2016 and in a few moments Phyllis would endorse Mr. Trump before thousands of enthusiastic supporters who were already making noise on the other side of the dressing room wall.

The conversation among the three of us was driven by Phyllis. She made two requests of him and he agreed to both.

"I spent decades making the Republican Party platform conservative," she said. "Pro-life, for military superiority, for the family, against big government and much more. And I need you to help me keep it conservative."

She handed him a copy of the 2012 Republican Party platform. Trump took it, opened it to a few pages, and said "I know, and I'll do it. You can count on it."

But Phyllis wasn't done.

"One more thing" she said. "I need you to pick judges - at every level - like Scalia and Thomas. It's important."

Trump nodded and said "I agree. I won't let you down on this. I promise."

* * *

President Trump has not let us down. At the Republican Convention in Cleveland, Trump's campaign adopted the most conservative platform in history. As President, Trump has cut funding to abortion, embraced military superiority and otherwise enacted conservative policies.

Even more importantly, he has especially delivered the promise he made to Phyllis with regard to judges. Starting with Neil Gorsuch on the Supreme Court, Trump's administration has methodically vetted, then nominated, well-qualified judges. The White House has carefully assisted the Senate in confirming these to the federal bench. This steadfast dedication to appointing conservative members of the judiciary, in itself, will transform—and, more to the point, protect—America in the coming decades.

The media can scarcely believe all that Trump is accomplishing. In fact, rather than cover his impressive list of accomplishments, they have chosen to focus on such things as the President's golfing or his tweets. In doing so, they are missing a monumental presidency.

Trump's record speaks for itself. **This book is a record of the promises he made AND then kept.** Most politicians say one thing and then do whatever else in office. Trump did what he said. On each page, you will find the proof of his promises made and kept. As you go through this list, you will realize that this is the greatest presidency since George Washington.

One more gift to you: the key speeches included in this volume indicate Trump's depth of understanding of where we are in the world and where we are going. Each lay out exactly what America First means: strong, vibrant, and encouraging. The phrase he uses—"a reawakening of nations"—will echo as a great one in history.

For those of us who believe what we see, it is clear we are making America great again! For those who disbelieve, I offer this book as an option for your future belief.

St. Louis, Missouri
September 1, 2020

Foreword by Corey R. Lewandowski

Over the years that I've known Mr. Donald J. Trump, there are two things I can count on: 1) he knows what he believes (and speaks his mind freely about what he believes!); and 2) when he gives you his word, you can take it to the bank. As President, Americans have seen up close what he did—and it's been great for America!

When I first met President Trump, I was amazed by his energy and by his focus on success for himself, his family, and those around him. When he decided to run for president, he added to his focus the one promise that Americans heard so often: to make America great again! What a difference he has made. He has pulled together so many of us—we the people—to get things going in a better direction.

One of the key people during the presidential campaign that President Trump sought to grow closer to was the late Phyllis Schlafly. Her ideas on American exceptionalism and especially on trade and immigration were so similar to President Trump we found ourselves watching for her weekly columns and interviews to hear how she gave voice to her support for President Trump. We were thrilled and honored when she endorsed Donald J. Trump for president!

In this book, Phyllis Schlafly's handpicked successor Ed Martin continues her work. He identifies the great successes by the Donald J. Trump presidency in his first term. From Kavanaugh to the return of American jobs to the near-peace in North Korea, it's hard to keep track of all the successes—it's good for us that Ed puts them all in this volume. This book includes special speeches by President Trump before the U.N. when he put the world on alert: America would always be first! Ed is right that these speeches capture all the essence of the America First movement.

Donald J. Trump ran for president not because he needed a job or a credential on his already outstanding resume. I heard him say in private meetings and in countless rallies: he ran because believes in the American people and in making America great again.

Even in the face of the great threats to us posed by the China Virus and the left's incessant attack, President Trump knows we will succeed—together. As we remember the many Promises Made, Promises Kept, let's work so that President Trump has so many more successes in his second term.

MAGA!

New Hampshire
September 2020

Promises Made

Promises Kept

Throughout the 2016 presidential campaign, Donald Trump cast his vision of renewed American greatness in the form of promises to the American people. So many elected officials had let the American people down before, but Donald Trump promised to be different.

The narrative of the mainstream media regarding Trump has not changed since the moment he announced his candidacy on June 16, 2015. The theme has always been Trump's reputation as a loose cannon and a free thinker. Paired with his history of never having held public office, the media hoped to destroy him before he could even have the chance to follow through on his promises.

Four years later, President Trump is no longer a man without a track record in public office. As the American people consider who is worthy of their vote in November, they must carefully consider not only what the candidates have said, but also what the candidates have done.

However, the purpose of this book is not merely to list out President Trump's accomplishments, but to disprove the assertion of the mainstream media that Trump is an unpredictable loose cannon. If anyone wants to know what he will do, they need only look at what he has promised. There is no shroud of mystery over his actions. Unlike almost every elected official in history, President Trump has followed through on his promises to the American people.

Promise #1
Make America Energy Independent

In 2016, candidate Donald Trump made clear that he would get us off foreign energy. He recognized the clear national security and economic need. As he saw it, American presidents had been supplicants to other energy-producing nations for far too long. They were weak! He promised to be strong.

Trump promised that we would not rule out any potential energy sources: of course coal, oil, and gas, but also nuclear, solar, wind, and hydroelectric. No option was off the table in his mission to make America energy independent. We could not afford to put all our eggs in one basket, whether that basket be fossil fuels, renewables, or something else. Supporting innovation to make new technologies more reliable was a major focus for him, but he did not forsake America's vital coal, oil, or natural gas industries either.

President Trump followed through on his promise in record time. He rapidly cut regulations so Americans could restart coal and fracking. He and his Energy Department encouraged rapid expansion into new fields including safe and efficient Generation IV Nuclear Power. Within just a few months, America was on its path to energy independence. By the end of 2018, the dream was realized. President Trump showed the world how to put American energy first so we didn't have to allow dictators in the Persian Gulf to hold us hostage. America is in charge of its energy and our future is bright.

Find out more about this Promise Kept by visiting PMPK2020.com

Promise #2
Jobs! Jobs! Jobs!

Donald Trump ran for president of the United States on a platform of American jobs first. True to his word, over three million people found jobs in just the first year and a half of his administration. For much of his tenure in office, there have been more jobs available than there have been people to fill them. Trump has taken bold and decisive action to give Americans the opportunity to get to work again. By dropping out of the TPP to take on China and renegotiating NAFTA into the USMCA, President Trump exercised his authority as chief diplomat to put American workers first. Those agreements would have outsourced even more jobs to foreign companies, selling America's manufacturing industry for the sake of appeasement and a few cheap goods. Even after the China virus shutdown, President Trump's optimism and policies curbed what could have been an even more catastrophic situation for American families. President Trump rapidly installed unemployment protection for American workers who were displaced by the China virus. His quick action gave desperate Americans what they needed to live until they could return to work again.

President Trump recognizes the simple fact that Americans need jobs. That's true in the middle of a pandemic just like it's true any other time. The numbers make it clear that President Trump has proven his commitment to make American jobs a priority.

Find out more about this Promise Kept by visiting PMPK2020.com

Promise #3
Americanism, Not Globalism, Will Be Our Credo

For far too long, Americans were sold out by leaders who chose serving the global elites over We the People. Globalists seek power for the ultra wealthy of all nations rather than supporting the ideals of a constitutional republic like the United States. Donald Trump ran for president saying he would always put the needs of American citizens first. He reiterated this promise in his famous 2017 speech in Poland and again in multiple addresses at the United Nations. He checked the power of the UN, dropped out of the Paris Climate Agreement, stopped bad multilateral deals, and defunded the corrupt World Health Organization. Ever the dealmaker, President Trump pointed out that America was paying far more than her fair share of dues to the North Atlantic Treaty Organization. After putting pressure on NATO and refusing to budge, they eventually caved by announcing a plan to make more nations pay more dues. Clearly, President Trump can't be bought by the allures of globalism.

As his ultimate response to globalism, Donald Trump stands up to the Chinese communists, who have tried to use globalism as a path to destroy our way of life. They do not simply steal our jobs. They actively steal American intellectual property with impunity.

Donald Trump stands in the shoes of George Washington, who made clear that the greatest service to the world is a strong America.

Find out more about this Promise Kept by visiting PMPK2020.com

Promise #4
Be A Great Champion Of Black Americans

For decades, the case of the famous black boxer Jack Johnson had been bandied about by politicians of every party and every race. Johnson had been wrongly imprisoned in 1912 for violating a law that hadn't gone into effect yet. Donald Trump pardoned Jack Johnson, which was something even Barack Obama didn't have the courage to do. Donald Trump enacted real criminal justice reform that has freed citizens of all colors, but especially black Americans. Donald Trump has also fought for increased spending for historically black colleges and universities. During the first years of his presidency, blacks were the prime beneficiaries of Trump's efforts to bring jobs to impoverished communities and black unemployment plummeted lower than it ever had before.

As the China virus swept through our nation, President Trump stepped up to protect the rights of children in black communities. He championed school choice for many parents who would find virtual learning to be difficult or impossible. Even in the midst of rampant rioting in American cities, President Trump has shown himself a friend of the thousands of law-abiding black business owners who were terrorized by the violent crimes in their streets. While preserving the autonomy of states and municipalities, Trump offered full support for black-owned businesses that were commonly targeted by rioters. President Donald Trump is a true friend to black Americans.

Find out more about this Promise Kept by visiting PMPK2020.com

Promise #5
Follow The Republican Party Platform

Some conservative were baffled when Phyllis Schlafly, founder of the modern pro-family movement, became one of the first true movement conservatives to endorse Donald Trump at a St. Louis rally on March 11, 2016. Many wondered what she knew that they did not. From the self-publication of her groundbreaking book *A Choice Not An Echo* in 1964, Phyllis Schlafly was a pioneer in backing strong conservative candidates, particularly for the Republican nomination for the presidency. Phyllis met privately with Trump before the rally, but she did not keep her reasons for endorsing him a secret. He personally promised her that he would follow the tenets of the Republican Party Platform. To Phyllis, that was everything. Deeply involved in every Republican Convention from 1952 to 2016, she had carefully worked for decades to keep the Platform conservative. She introduced the first pro-life language into the Platform. In her mind, the Platform was the voice of conservative grassroots activists throughout the nation. When Donald Trump promised to follow it, she believed him.

From cutting taxes and regulation to promoting the Constitution and American exceptionalism, Donald Trump has kept his commitment to the conservative values embodied in the Republican Party Platform. Never Trumpers claimed Trump was a liberal in disguise, but he has done more to codify the conservative values of the Platform than any other president in modern history.

Find out more about this Promise Kept by visiting PMPK2020.com

Promise #6
Bomb ISIS

As Donald Trump was running for office in 2016, ISIS was running rampant in the Middle East. Weak political leadership from the Obama administration facilitated the rapid spread of the dangerous caliphate known for cursing America and beheading journalists, aid workers, and Christians. At the height of their power, they held territory in Yemen, Saudia Arabia, Egypt, Libya, Afghanistan, Nigeria, Pakistan, and Algeria. More than ten million souls were in subjection to their evil reign of terror. Trump saw the terrible mistakes being made by America's commander-in-chief and vowed to bomb ISIS into submission. Sure enough, President Trump had barely taken office when he ordered a substantial increase in the bombing of ISIS targets. Our brave military men and women dropped bombs like the great GBU-43 on ISIS tunnels to deny their ability to operate successfully and to show the world that America meant business. The GBU-43 is the largest non-nuclear bomb in America's arsenal.

Just as candidate Trump had predicted, ISIS rapidly lost territory and power. While they have not completely disappeared, almost all of their territory has been stripped from them. President Trump's abilities as a commander-in-chief prove he has what it takes to handle the biggest bullies in the world and win. He does not shy away from taking big action to address a big problem. Don't believe me? Just ask ISIS, or at least what's left of it.

Find out more about this Promise Kept by visiting PMPK2020.com

Promise #7
Bring Back "Merry Christmas"

Americans may forget how Donald Trump's candidacy began with his commitment to push back on the dangerous culture of political correctness that plagued our nation. The ultimate example of this culture war is the prevalence of Scrooges who fight to keep the words "Merry Christmas" out of town squares, businesses, and the mouths of the American people. Ever the social justice warrior, President Obama chose to wish people a happy "holiday" on the official White House Christmas card during his administration. When President Trump took office, he remedied this situation by prominently wishing Americans a "Merry Christmas and a Happy New Year" in the 2017 White House Christmas card. In both subsequent cards, he made sure the word "Christmas" wasn't cut. In speeches and other public appearances, President Trump has boldly proclaimed yuletide wishes to all.

President Trump brought back Merry Christmas, but he also brought back a celebration of the Judeo-Christian holiday enjoyed by every citizen in the United States. America's religious roots are nothing to be ashamed of. Trump does not shy away from celebrating the faith of all Americans. He also didn't shy away from making clear that religious communities of all stripes must have the freedom to worship and to live out their faith according to their conscience. President Trump has never stopped saying what he truly believes. He does not plan on muzzling other Americans during the Christmas season either.

Find out more about this Promise Kept by visiting PMPK2020.com

Promise #8
Bring Back Coal Mining Jobs

Failed candidate Hillary Clinton made a terrible mistake when she arrogantly boasted that she wanted to "put a lot of coal miners and coal companies out of business." Most Democrat candidates up to that point were at least smart enough not to admit their hatred of coal workers out loud, even though their policies said as much. Hillary did not care to hide her disdain for these hardworking Americans. President Trump made sure Americans knew he didn't share Clinton's animosity. In fact, he promised to bring back the coal jobs Clinton's party had tried so desperately to destroy. As Donald Trump took office, there were two major threats to America's coal industry: the environmental activists and overbearing regulatory agencies. President Trump took on both of these groups by cutting regulations at a record pace. After less than a month in office, he signed H.J. Resolution 38 to eliminate unnecessary rules that did nothing but hurt American companies employing thousands of coal miners.

President Trump's actions didn't stop there. He continues to be a voice for coal workers, bringing many to the Republican Party who had traditionally voted Democrat. Hillary Clinton may have wanted to put lots of coal miners out of a job, but she found out the hard way that if you don't back miners like Trump did, the office of the presidency is one job you won't be offered.

Find out more about this Promise Kept by visiting PMPK2020.com

Promise #9
Bring Back The American Dream

For too long American leaders in Washington kept expanding their power and diminishing the American dream. President Trump made clear that the special interests would not dominate him because he didn't come from their politics and didn't need their money. The American dream, for many, comes down to opportunity and freedom. Americans want the opportunity to get a job and work hard. Americans want to have doors open to them. Americans want to have the freedom to choose what they think is best for themselves and their families. Simply put, they want the autonomy to manage their own lives.

When President Trump historically cut taxes for nearly all American citizens and businesses, he created opportunity by encouraging new businesses to launch and empowering existing businesses to grow. He promoted freedom by letting Americans have more control over their own paychecks. With that control, individuals can make financial decisions for the betterment of their families rather than trusting the government for more handouts. The American dream is alive and well in President Trump's America. With hard work, determination, and prudent decision making, anyone can rise up from their circumstances and seize a better life. Trump did not do the hard work for you, but he got government out of the way so you could do the work yourself. All Americans need is the courage to seize the American dream as they see it.

Find out more about this Promise Kept by visiting PMPK2020.com

Promises #10
Bring Jobs Back From Overseas

On June 1, 2016, President Barack Obama infamously said that some jobs "are just not going to come back." Thankfully, Donald Trump did not agree with Obama's defeatism. Instead, he chose to believe in the power of American industry to surge above and beyond the heights it enjoyed in years past. Trump promised to bring jobs back to America again. Obama scoffed that there is "no answer" to getting the jobs back, and that Trump would need a "magic wand" to do it.

As it turns out, the "magic wand" is as simple as creating a climate in which manufacturers know they will prosper. President Trump lowered the corporate tax rate from 35% to 21%, which took America from far above to far below the international average. As a result, the jobs started pouring back in. Big companies like Apple, Boeing, General Motors, Dow Chemical, and Whirlpool added tens of thousands of jobs in states like Michigan, Louisiana, Missouri, South Carolina, New York, and Tennessee. The career politicians like President Obama want to fool Americans into accepting that manufacturing jobs can never come back to America, but President Trump is a businessman who knows better. He knew how to draw in manufacturers, and he followed through. It didn't take a magic wand to bring back American jobs, just a president with strong conservative principles and the boldness to follow through with them.

Find out more about this Promise Kept by visiting PMPK2020.com

Promise #11
Bring Troops Home

Candidate Trump knew the American people were tired of being entangled in the affairs of other nations. He promised that he would withdraw our troops from Syria. Of course, that would not have been possible without getting rid of ISIS's deathgrip in the region. After President Trump followed through with his promises to bomb and rapidly defeat ISIS, it became possible to make his promise to withdraw our troops a reality. In fact, he sent a tweet on December 19, 2018 saying, "We have defeated ISIS in Syria, my only reason for being there during the Trump Presidency." Shortly thereafter, he directed the Pentagon to begin making this a reality. Despite loud protestations from Trump's usual critics, it is clear that this did not diminish our policy of American military superiority. White House Press Secretary Sarah Sanders assured the American people that, "We have started returning United States troops home as we transition to the next phase of this campaign. The United States and our allies stand ready to re-engage at all levels to defend American interests whenever necessary."

President Trump was smart to follow through on his campaign promise to bring the troops home. There is no reason to risk the lives of America's men and women in uniform fighting endless wars in the Middle East. When Trump eliminated the threat of ISIS, it was time to come home.

Find out more about this Promise Kept by visiting PMPK2020.com

Promise #12
Build The Wall

All Americans remember the chants from Trump's 2016 campaign pleading for him to "Build That Wall!" In many ways, building a wall along the southern border became Trump's signature issue. As such, opponents of President Trump have stopped at nothing to prevent the wall from being built. Think about it: the Democrats started complaining about something being a waste of taxpayer money. They really must have been desperate! Defending the interests of taxpayers has never been their forte. Despite the overbearing opposition and intervening crises like COVID-19, more than two hundred and fifty miles of border wall have been built as of this writing. Constructing these sturdy sections of thirty-foot-high border wall has used around three hundred thousand tons of steel and six hundred thousand cubic yards of concrete. The construction is ongoing, so check with the U.S. Customs and Border Protection website for the latest totals.

There's a reason for all those "Build That Wall" chants. Americans are tired of people breaking the rules to come to this nation. Nobody likes a rule breaker. If someone would like to be a part of the greatest nation on Earth, let them file for a visa like everyone else. America doesn't want unvetted people streaming across the border to steal jobs, endanger citizens, and use valuable resources. The rapidly rising wall is a symbol to the rest of the world of America's demand that everyone respect the rule of law within our borders.

Find out more about this Promise Kept by visiting PMPK2020.com

Promise #13
Cancel Visas To Countries That Won't Take Back Illegals

Candidate Donald Trump's Contract With The American Voter promised that he would not only deport criminal illegal aliens, but that he would "cancel visas to foreign countries that won't take them back." It only makes sense. If a dangerous criminal passes illegally from another nation into the United States, it's not the job of the American taxpayer to take on the expense of their care. Their country of origin should take them back and deal with them. However, some nations routinely refused to take their criminals back. Candidate Trump promised this would come to an end. Sure enough, the Trump administration issued visa sanctions against Sierra Leone, Eritrea, Cambodia, and Guinea. Not only does this put pressure on those nations, but it also serves as a strong warning to the rest of the world that America will not act as an international babysitter for the world's criminals. Every nation must be responsible for their own citizens, just as the United States is for theirs.

The rest of the world had taken advantage of America's goodwill for decades before President Trump came on the scene. Other presidents were either too intimidated to take a stand, or else they simply did not care about the problem. It took a man of bold conviction and an iron will to stand up against these international bullies. Once again, Trump proved he would follow through on his promises to the American people.

Find out more about this Promise Kept by visiting PMPK2020.com

Promise #14
Clear The Way For The Keystone Pipeline

The Keystone XL pipeline was first proposed in 2005 as a common sense solution to the problem of transporting crude oil from Canada down to the Gulf Coast. The project quickly became mired in politics and environmentalists sued over and over to block the construction of this tremendously valuable economic tool. The Obama administration actively worked against it, and eventually vetoed it outright, saying that it wasn't in the "national interest" despite the fact that it would generate thousands of new jobs. Candidate Trump vowed to reverse course on this terrible mistake. After just two months in office, President Trump gave approval for the project to move forward and then pushed again in 2019 to fasttrack the construction process, saying that, "Keystone XL will have a limited effect on the environment." The radical environmentalists may not have been happy, but workers throughout the oil industry cheered. TransCanada president Russ Girling loudly voiced his approval saying, "The Keystone XL pipeline has been studied more than any other pipeline in history, and the environmental reviews are clear—the project can be built and operated in an environmentally sustainable and responsible way."

While we have to be good stewards of our planet, bogging down a vital economic generator on frivolous grounds is not in America's best interest. President Trump was right to allow this important project to move forward. American progress has been held captive long enough.

Find out more about this Promise Kept by visiting PMPK2020.com

Promise #15
Create A Private Hotline For Veterans

It is no big secret that the Department of Veterans Affairs (VA) has not always lived up to its mission of providing veterans with the care and assistance they need. Speaking to the Veterans of Foreign Wars National Convention on July 26, 2016, candidate Donald Trump promised to "create a private White House Hotline—that is answered by a real person 24 hours a day—to make sure that no valid complaint about the VA ever falls through the cracks." He went on to say "If a valid complaint is not acted upon, then the issue will be brought directly to me, and I will pick up the phone and fix it myself, if need be."

For most candidates for public office, this would be an empty promise quickly tossed aside once the election was won. For Donald Trump, making a promise means getting it done. He followed through on his bold promise to the letter. The hotline was launched in June 2017. By October, it was fully staffed with 90% of the team being either veterans themselves or those with veteran family members. In less than two months, the hotline had served more than ten thousand callers. This very moment, any veteran with a complaint about the Department of Veterans Affairs can call 855-948-2311 and speak with a real person about the problem. President Trump doesn't just give lip service to supporting veterans. He follows through on his promises.

Promise #16
Create Tax Atmosphere Favoring Middle Class Americans

Candidate Donald Trump's plan to bolster the economy was as effective as it was simple. He promised to ease the tax burden on middle class Americans by letting them "keep more money in their pockets and increase after-tax wages." Of course, just about every candidate running as a Republican makes the exact same promise. The difference with President Trump is that he actually put in the hard work to get it done.

2017's iconic Tax Cuts and Jobs Act was the ultimate fulfillment of this promise. The Heritage Foundation released a report proclaiming that the average American family will pocket an extra $45,000 over the next decade as a result of this piece of legislation. Imagine what hardworking American families can do with an extra $45,000. This crucial tax cut provides the upward mobility that America is famous for. Middle class Americans benefited from the new law because of the doubled child care tax credit and the nearly doubled standard deduction, not to mention the substantially lowered middle tax brackets. The iconic words "life, liberty, and pursuit of happiness" speak to the ability for all men and women to reach their greatest potential through hard work and dedication. That's what conservatism is all about. Donald Trump championed conservative principles on the campaign trail and didn't leave them at the door of the White House on his way in.

Find out more about this Promise Kept by visiting PMPK2020.com

Promise #17
Cut Corporate Tax Rate

Prior to the Tax Cuts and Jobs Act of 2017, the maximum corporate tax rate in the United States was 35%. This high tax rate made it difficult for American businesses to launch and thrive. Even worse, that rate was among the highest in the world, making it difficult for American companies to compete in the global market. As a result, many companies either moved overseas or just shut down completely. It is hard to keep a business on American shores when the American government acts like it does not want the business there. Candidate Trump promised to lower the corporate tax rate to remedy these problems.

He kept that promise in the very first year of his presidency. The Tax Cuts and Jobs Act permanently changed the corporate tax rate from 35% to a mind-blowing 21%. To put that in context, the corporate tax rate hasn't been lower than 21% since the beginning of World War II. Today's American entrepreneurs can start businesses with confidence knowing their tax rates will stay low under President Trump. Major domestic corporations can compete globally. It's no wonder small business confidence and consumer confidence have maintained historic highs throughout much of President Trump's first term. President Trump knows exactly what these American ventures need to perform with peak efficiency. Businesses know that they can thrive under the administration of a true businessman-president.

Find out more about this Promise Kept by visiting PMPK2020.com

Promise #18
Cut Taxes For All

As was previously mentioned, the Tax Cuts and Jobs Act of 2017 was highly beneficial for the middle class and for businesses of all stripes. However, that wasn't where the tax cuts stopped. The rates were lowered, the standard deduction was doubled, and the Obamacare tax penalty was eliminated. Not only did President Trump cut taxes for the middle class, but for ninety percent of all Americans regardless of their tax bracket.

Democrats actually tried to use this as a weapon against Trump, saying that the bill was all about helping the wealthy. The bill certainly did cut taxes for the wealthy, but it cut taxes for everyone else too. Helping one group doesn't mean the other can't be helped at the same time. Tax cuts do not have have to be a zero-sum game. When Democrats say they would not have cut taxes for the rich, they might be telling the truth. However, what they won't say is that they certainly would not have cut taxes for the middle class either.

Even if someone doesn't fall among the 90% who experienced a direct cut to their personal tax bill, everyone of all economic classes benefits from the lowered corporate tax rate. Major corporations like Walmart, AT&T, and Wells Fargo passed these tax savings directly on to employees in the form of bonuses. President Trump's Tax Cuts and Jobs Act was an important tax cut for all Americans.

Find out more about this Promise Kept by visiting PMPK2020.com

Promise #19
Declare China A Currency Manipulator

Currency manipulation might not be the most trendy political issue, but it has a tangible effect on every American. A nation is a currency manipulator if they intentionally decrease the value of their own currency to leverage better trade with another nation. China decreased the value of the yuan by 1.4% in a single day. When American retailers went to buy Chinese products, they had to pay 1.4% more to get the same amount of goods. When put in the context of hundreds of billions of dollars, this is not chump change. Obviously, there's nothing "free" about that kind of free trade. China had previously committed to not manipulate currency as a member of the G20, but they went back on their word. Americans essentially had to pay that extra cost as they would any other tax.

President Trump promised to "bring China to the bargaining table" by declaring it a currency manipulator. Sure enough, he declared China a currency manipulator immediately after their intentional 1.4% decline. That official designation triggered a series of punitive actions which increased pressure on China. Even though China's currency manipulation is nothing new, the U.S. had not declared them or anyone else an official currency manipulator since 1994. This kind of bold and innovative thinking is exactly why America needs President Trump to continue making deals for the United States.

Find out more about this Promise Kept by visiting PMPK2020.com

Promise #20
Decrease Wasteful Spending

During his acceptance speech at the 2016 Republican National Convention in Cleveland, Donald Trump said, "We are going to ask every department head in government to provide a list of wasteful spending projects that we can eliminate in my first 100 days. The politicians have talked about this for years, but I'm going to do it." He knew Americans were tired of funneling trillions of their hard-earned tax dollars into a deeply-entrenched bureaucratic nightmare. Plenty of other candidates had capitalized on this same frustration with empty promises on the campaign trail, but President Trump followed through.

On January 23, 2017, a mere three days after taking office, President Trump ordered a three-month hiring freeze on federal employees. He cut a mountain of unnecessary paper-pushing positions out of key departments. The Education Department cut 15% of their employees. The State Department cut 11%. Even 15% of IRS agent positions were eliminated. Many of these cuts were offset by additions to the Department of Veterans Affairs and the Department of Homeland Security, but that's exactly what Trump ran on. He promised to cut wasteful spending, take care of our veterans, and hire more Border Patrol agents. His targeted cuts fulfill key promises Donald Trump ran on. His level-headed approach to governance has saved Americans untold billions of tax dollars which would have otherwise disappeared into the D.C. Swamp.

Find out more about this Promise Kept by visiting PMPK2020.com

Promise #21
Defeat The Establishment

They say the definition of insanity is doing the same thing over and over while expecting a different result. Candidate Donald Trump promised to give America something different from the same parade of career politicians. As a businessman in New York City, Trump certainly knew how politicians operated. However, having never held an elected office himself, it was clear that he was an outsider running entirely separate from the political Establishment. Not even President Trump's opponents accuse him of being anybody's puppet. In fact, they paint him as being a dangerous maverick with nothing to hold him back. Career politicians are so used to receiving their orders from the Establishment that they are not comfortable with someone who actually fights on behalf of the American people.

They attacked Trump with everything they had, but the Establishment fell to the might of We The People when Donald Trump was elected. They still try to tear him down however they can, but now America knows they can be defeated if patriots are willing to stand strong behind a true fighter. Although President Trump is willing to work with anyone who shares his goals, he is not beholden to the will of the Establishment. The only group he answers to is the American people. Clearly, Trump's defeat of the Establishment in 2016 was a victory for the nation and all who live in it.

Promise #22
Defeat The Never Trumpers

As candidate Donald Trump was working to overcome the Establishment in an unprecedented grassroots wave, a small insurgency posing as conservatives loudly worked against Trump's true conservative efforts. The people in this insurgency became known as "Never Trumpers." The title fit well, because they stubbornly refused to support Trump, even when the only other alternative was the pro-abortion globalist Hillary Clinton. Some actively worked on Clinton's behalf in a clear betrayal of their conservative roots. Others tried to pull votes away from Trump for a third party candidate, which was just as good as handing votes to Hillary. Trump promised to win for the American people in spite of this opposition from supposed "conservatives."

Not only did Donald Trump go on to win the presidency, but he also continued to make Never Trumpers less and less influential with time. As the American people saw the strong conservative leadership of President Trump, it became clearer and clearer that an absolutist position against Trump would only be a victory for the radical left. Undoubtedly, the Never Trumpers command very little respect today. Four Never Trumpers tried vainly to primary Trump for the 2020 nomination, garnering a single delegate to Trump's 2,367. Without question, it is clear to see the Never Trump movement has been very thoroughly defeated at the hands of the conservative Donald Trump.

Find out more about this Promise Kept by visiting PMPK2020.com

Promise #23
Defend South Korea

Immediately after the November 2016 election, President Trump promised South Korean President Park Geun-hye that he would make Korea's defense a top priority in his administration. Perhaps even President-elect Trump didn't know how much pressure he would be under to break that promise. The Trump administration had barely begun when North Korean Dictator Kim Jong-Un began ramping up ballistic missile testing amid loud threats to any would-be aggressors. Obviously, this was a grave threat to the entire world, but to South Korea in particular. President Trump refused to cave to pressure from North Korea. He gave Kim the nickname "Little Rocket Man" and declared that any aggression from the Hermit Kingdom would "be met with fire and fury like the world has never seen." North Korea continued to sabre-rattle, even launching an ICBM which landed in the Sea of Japan. When these options were exhausted, Kim Jong-Un finally came to the negotiating table with President Trump.

While the story of Korean-American relations is far from over, it is undeniable that President Trump has invested considerable effort and political capital to protect South Korea and the world from the threats of North Korea. Even as President Trump has pressured South Korea to pay their fair share for military aid, they have remained a stalwart ally because they know Trump is on their side. He is a stalwart defender of America and her close allies.

Find out more about this Promise Kept by visiting PMPK2020.com

Promise #24
Defund Planned Parenthood

At the 2016 Republican primary debate in Houston, Donald Trump said, "I would defund [Planned Parenthood] because of the abortion factor, which they say is 3 percent. I don't know what percentage it is. They say it's 3 percent. But I would defund it, because I'm pro-life." After being elected to the presidency, Trump didn't forget his promise to the millions of pro-life Americans who pleaded for action. One can't say the same for the Republican House and Senate elected with President Trump in 2016. These so-called "pro-life" Republicans totally dropped the ball when they had the best chance in years to fully defund the nation's largest abortion provider. However, President Trump didn't shrug his shoulders and give up when Congress caved. Trump instructed his Department of Health and Human Services to cut all Title X funding to organizations providing abortions. His goal was to stop federal dollars from going to abortion providers, not just to punish a hated group. The new HHS rules graciously offered to keep giving money to Planned Parenthood if they were willing to stop providing abortions. Predictably, Planned Parenthood announced that they would no longer draw money from the $286 million Title X program. Apparently that "3%" is really important to them.

The fight against Planned Parenthood continues, but President Trump has certainly done his part by dealing a massive blow to the nation's largest abortion giant.

Find out more about this Promise Kept by visiting PMPK2020.com

Promise #25
Deport Criminal Illegal Aliens

Donald Trump built his presidential campaign on the mantra of "America First." The idea is simple: national policy should never hurt Americans and give unfair preference to non-Americans. In line with this mantra, Trump announced at a rally in Miami that "A Trump administration will stop illegal immigration, deport all criminal aliens, and save American lives." As though echoing the sentiments of the entire nation, the crowd erupted in cheers. As soon as President Trump took office, he set about to tackle the threat of criminal aliens with the full force of the United States government. He hired more Immigrations and Customs Enforcement (ICE) agents and stood with them. In just two years, ICE arrested nearly three times as many suspected gang members as in 2016. The number of suspected terrorists apprehended skyrocketed. In total, more than 27,000 more illegals with criminal histories were arrested in 2018 than in 2016.

America has no obligation to act as a receptacle for the world's criminals. If they endanger innocent Americans, they should be immediately returned to their country of origin. That is the logic Donald Trump ran for the presidency on, and that is the policy President Trump implemented. The numbers don't lie. Trump has consistently committed his administration to the removal of dangerous criminal illegal aliens. "America First" means protecting the American people from criminal aliens.

Find out more about this Promise Kept by visiting PMPK2020.com

Promise #26
Do A Great Job For Our Nation

Candidate Donald Trump promised that he would work tirelessly for the American people. Being a man with a strong background in the realm of business, he treated the campaign like a job interview. He listed his qualifications, laid out a vision, and set his resume down before the American people. We The People hired Trump for the job because we believed he would do the job well. Without a doubt, President Trump was met with resistance at every turn. From the Democrats' refusal to accept the results of the election to the violent demonstrations on his Inauguration Day, liberals made it clear that they would oppose his every move. They carried out an endless parade of contrived scandal, featuring the Russia collusion hoax, the nomination nightmare of Justice Brett Kavanaugh, and the impeachment sham. Despite all this, President Donald Trump persists. He has fought endlessly for the rights of Americans. In his first year alone, the Heritage Foundation estimated that he had completed 64% of the agenda he ran on. By their calculations, that even put him ahead of President Ronald Reagan at the same point in his presidency.

The American people wanted a fighter and that's exactly what we got. President Trump has done the job he was hired to do. As an employee of We the People, he has performed far above and beyond every expectation. I would say he should get a raise, but he won't even take a salary!

Find out more about this Promise Kept by visiting PMPK2020.com

Promise #27
Drain The Swamp

In a speech in 1982, President Reagan recalled the old saying "when you're up to your armpits in alligators, it's sometimes hard to remember that your original intention was to drain the swamp." Candidate Donald Trump used the phrase "drain the swamp" to define his own crusade against the entrenched bureaucrats in the Washington, D.C. beltway. It didn't take long before the chant became a hallmark of any Trump campaign event. Thankfully, despite the alligators that constantly snap at his presidency, President Trump has not forgotten his mission to drain the swamp. He brought on a Cabinet that shares his vision for making deep cuts into the bureaucracy, then he set them loose to make those cuts. Key departments of the Executive eliminated large numbers of positions, such as the Departments of Education, Treasury, and State. Additionally, President Trump issued Executive Order 13770 one week after taking office. This order banned employees of the Executive from becoming lobbyists for five years after leaving the administration. When it comes to the plush government employee unions, Trump is not intimidated. He knows he works for We The People, not well-funded special interests.

President Trump's work to drain the swamp is not over yet, but he has taken every measure possible to combat the corruption our nation's capital is known for. The Trump administration is fighting the swamp creatures for We The People.

Find out more about this Promise Kept by visiting PMPK2020.com

Promise #28
End DACA And DAPA

Candidate Donald Trump promised to eliminate two of President Obama's signature policies called Deferred Action for Parents of Americans and Lawful Permanent Residents (DAPA) and Deferred Action for Childhood Arrivals (DACA.) The purpose of DAPA was to provide a citizenship path for illegal immigrants whose children are American citizens. DACA was to provide a citizenship path for illegal immigrants brought to America as minors. Trump contended that United States citizenship should not be carelessly handed out to someone who came to America illegally. Instead, first consideration should be given to those who seek to come to America legally. Both DAPA and DACA were created by executive order under President Obama. Constitutionally, President Trump should have full authority to rescind both, so that's precisely what he did in 2017. While the DAPA rescission has remained intact, the Trump administration was sued to keep DACA in place. After a three-year legal battle, the Supreme Court ignored the clear text of the Constitution and ruled that Trump could not end DACA the same way President Obama started it.

Since that time, President Trump's DHS announced that they will not receive new DACA applications as they reconsider the future of the program. As acting DHS Secretary Chad Wolf said in a statement, "There are important policy reasons that may warrant the full rescission of the DACA policy."

Find out more about this Promise Kept by visiting PMPK2020.com

Promise #29
Expand Healthcare For Our Veterans

The Department of Veterans Affairs (VA) is absolutely infamous for inefficiency and mismanagement. Not long ago, veterans had to drive hours upon hours to reach an approved doctor after waiting weeks and weeks just to get an appointment. It was truly a national disgrace for our brave and honorable veterans to be treated so poorly by their own government. Candidate Donald Trump promised to open up new doors for veterans so they could get the healthcare they deserve. This promise was delivered with the VA MISSION Act of 2018. The act took a multi-pronged approach to bettering healthcare services for our nation's heroes. First and most importantly, it combines several private-care programs to make the process much easier for a veteran to receive care from a non-VA medical facility. Second, it expands the capability of the VA by incentivizing the hiring of new staff and by more wisely directing the construction and repair of VA facilities. Third, it expands the ability of the VA to cover in-home care for veterans who need it.

The VA MISSION Act is a clear example of President Trump delivering for the American people. We all saw the problems with the VA, but it took someone with independence and grit to push a solution through the muck and mire of the Washington, D.C. bureaucracy. President Trump is the first president in a long time with the political will to get things done.

Find out more about this Promise Kept by visiting PMPK2020.com

Promise #30
Expand Our Navy To 350 Ships

Candidate Donald Trump was very clear and specific about his goals for the United States military. He promised to "build a Navy of 350 surface ships and submarines as recommended by the bipartisan National Defense Panel." This kind of noble goal is exactly what America should be focusing on. The United States absolutely must maintain military superiority in a new age of threats like communist China. To let America's domestic policy cloud the ability to defend American interests throughout the globe would be a tragic mistake. Our naval power in particular has been dramatically declining since the Reagan administration. Just from the decade of 1987 to 1997, the size of our fleet decreased by a whopping 40%. That is totally unacceptable by itself, but the numbers have only gotten worse since that time.

In the 2018 Defense Authorization Act, the Trump administration set out a national plan to achieve a goal of 355 ships, five ships more than his campaign promise. The act called for a gradual buildup of our fleet over the course of several decades, but tangible progress has already been made. When President Trump took office, the Navy had a total of 274 ships. At present, they have 299. The final goal of 355 is still a long way off, but Trump's administration has put America on the right track to maintaining our critical military superiority. America's ship hasn't sailed yet.

Find out more about this Promise Kept by visiting PMPK2020.com

Promise #31
Fix The System To Be Just For Every American

Criminal justice reform is an empty campaign promise to many political candidates. However, when Donald Trump promised criminal justice reform, he really meant it. In December 2018, he signed the First Step Act, a landmark criminal justice bill meant to benefit prison guards, prisoners transitioning back into society, and the American public. It established new guidelines for the U.S. Attorney General to tackle the exacting problem of recidivism. The blight of our criminal justice system, recidivism is defined as the likelihood of a criminal released from prison to go out and commit other crimes.

Furthermore, the First Step Act creates new guidelines to enforce the right of prison guards to carry concealed weapons outside prison facilities and to protect the health of pregnant and postpartum inmates. Sentencing reform was also addressed, along with provisions to give better training to guards, place inmates in prisons closer to their families, and improve reporting on drug use in prison.

Support for the First Step Act was widely bipartisan. President Trump's direction in this legislation makes a strong case for his leadership abilities. Clearly, he has what it takes to work with others for the benefit of the American people. He isn't just working on behalf of a few friends or a certain class of people. He is a champion of the rights of all Americans of every class, creed, sex, and pigmentation.

Promise #32
Fund Historically Black Colleges And Universities

The liberal media don't want America to know it, but President Trump is a stalwart champion of Historically Black Colleges and Universities (HBCUs). On the campaign trail, he promised to make them a top priority in his administration. Many people who had been saturated with leftwing propaganda assumed that this was just a vain attempt to win the votes of black Americans, but that proved not to be the case. Within two months of taking office, President Trump signed an executive order moving the HBCU initiative from the Department of Education to the White House. President Reagan had created the HBCU initiative in 1981, but President George W. Bush transferred it to the Education Department in 2002. By moving the initiative back to the White House, President Trump brought their voice closer to his administration and to the ears of the American people. And President Trump's actions did not stop with the transferal of one advisory board but took a much more substantive form. He proudly signed legislation increasing funding for HBCUs by an impressive 13%.

Of course, this flies in the face of everything America hears from the mainstream media. They do not want black Americans to know what President Trump is doing to help them. Instead, the media wants black Americans to think their president hates them. However, with an increase of funding that large, President Trump certainly has a funny way of showing it.

Find out more about this Promise Kept by visiting PMPK2020.com

Promise #33
Get Brett Kavanaugh Confirmed

There have been few times of greater political pressure and upheaval than during the hearings to confirm Brett Kavanaugh to the United States Supreme Court. Desperate liberals pushed a suspiciously unsubstantiated narrative to force President Trump to back down from his chosen appointee. Hyperbolic words filled the news as protestors filled the streets and Capitol offices calling for senators to relinquish their support for Judge Kavanaugh. Our Founding Fathers may have supported the right to peacefully assemble and petition for the redress of grievance, but they never meant for the confirmation process to take such a dark turn. Senate committees should not serve the function of our court system by trying appointees for alleged crimes. Of course, Democrats could not have taken their complaints to actual courts because clear evidentiary standards could never be met in a case against Kavanaugh.

So Democrats took a play out of their playbook from the nomination of Justice Clarence Thomas. They called in an alleged victim and put on the pressure in the largest political circus of the year, complete with plenty of clowns and contortionists. Thankfully, President Trump never gave up on Kavanaugh. He very easily could have picked a more liberal judicial supremacist to appoint to the High Court, but he chose to weather the storm so our courts could not be used as a political weapon to overrule the will of the American people.

Find out more about this Promise Kept by visiting PMPK2020.com

Promise #34
Get Out Of TPP

President Barack Obama considered the creation of the Trans-Pacific Partnership (TPP) to be one of the signature legacy items from his administration. The only problem was that TPP was a terrible deal for the American people. It would have ended thousands of American jobs as more and more manufacturing moved overseas. In fact, the deal was so bad that candidate Donald Trump was joined in his opposition to the deal by none other than Hillary Clinton and Bernie Sanders. Everyone knew it was a bad idea. However, Donald Trump is the one who followed through on his promise to "issue a notification of intent to withdraw from the Trans-Pacific Partnership." After only three days in office, President Trump gave official notification that America was pulling out of TPP. President Trump's reasoning for withdrawing goes beyond the terms of this one arrangement. He has always voiced a strong preference for bilateral trade deals rather than multilateral ones. With a bilateral deal, one can negotiate freely with one other party and find the best solution for both. If the other party doesn't follow the deal, it is relatively easy to pull out. However, if multiple nations are negotiating the deal, it becomes harder to get favorable terms or to pull out if a nation is not holding up to their end of the deal.

President Trump is a dealmaker at heart. There's a reason he pulled out of TPP by the third day of his administration. He's putting the American people first.

Find out more about this Promise Kept by visiting PMPK2020.com

Promise #35
Get Rid Of The Marriage Penalty

When most people think about getting married, they think about love, devotion, and a big white cake. Many do not think about the tax implications of getting married. However, before the Tax Cuts and Jobs Act of 2017, countless Americans were saddled with an extra tax burden for the crime of being married. This "marriage penalty" made no sense at all. There is no benefit to our communities or our nation to discourage marriage. In fact, the incentive should go in exactly the opposite direction. The institution of marriage is under attack, but it is still the best way to create an effective economic unit and a nurturing environment in which to raise children. If anything, tax laws should encourage marriage, not discourage it. Candidate Donald Trump promised to remove the marriage penalty from the United States tax code. In the Tax Cuts and Jobs Act, he did just that for most Americans. Aside from a few rare exceptions in the highest tax bracket, all Americans should see an end to their annual punishment for being married.

President Trump was wise to follow through with this. Studies show that households with a married husband and wife outperform their unmarried counterparts on most matrices. Married couples are far less likely to live below the poverty line or take government handouts. The United States government should not create a financial burden for pursuing the healthiest, most socially positive option.

Find out more about this Promise Kept by visiting PMPK2020.com

Promise #36
Give Dr. Ben Carson A Place In His Administration

Dr. Ben Carson is an exemplary person and an inspiration to millions. His story is a testament to the opportunity afforded to every person born in America, regardless of their background or circumstances. He ran a valiant campaign for the Republican nomination in 2016. Though he did not win against Donald Trump, the eventual nominee did promise to give Dr. Carson an important place in his administration. Sure enough, President Trump tapped Dr. Carson to serve as the Secretary for Housing and Urban Development. Given his uniquely humble background, this was the ideal place for Dr. Carson to use his gifts for the betterment of our nation. His unmatched intellect is useful as he works to meet the housing needs of America's poorest communities. His silent but stalwart convictions have been useful as he wades into the cesspool of political correctness to make sound policy. His department issued new guidance to support homeless shelters who want to accept people on the basis of their biological sex. In other words, Dr. Carson has assured womens shelters that they don't have to take in a homeless male just because he says he feels like a female. They have the power to refer that individual to a different shelter for men. Under President Obama, shelters were forced to bunk battered women right alongside strange men without question.

President Trump is doing the right thing by surrounding himself with wise counsellors like Dr. Ben Carson.

Find out more about this Promise Kept by visiting PMPK2020.com

Promise #37
Give Economic Prosperity To Hispanic Communities

When candidate Donald Trump announced his plan to stand boldly against illegal immigration, the mainstream media presumed he would forever be tarnished in the eyes of the Hispanic community. When he promised to be the best choice for Hispanic voters as well as everyone else, the media scoffed. After all, creating economic prosperity for minorities didn't fit in with their false narrative of hatred and bigotry. They wanted to portray Trump as only caring about the economic prosperity of rich white people. Thankfully, the media's attempts to whitewash history failed miserably. True to his word, President Trump delivered for Hispanic voters by achieving record low unemployment for them, as well as for black Americans. The media just did not understand that Hispanic Americans need jobs too. They don't want the problems of illegal immigration any more than the rest of the nation does. In fact, American citizens in the Hispanic community are actually more likely to be negatively impacted by illegal immigrants. If illegal workers take all of the low wage jobs, they are not leaving opportunities for the good people who came to America legally in search of the chance to build a better life for their families.

President Trump truly is a champion for the Hispanic community. His policies encourage economic growth at all levels, but particularly for middle and lower class Americans who are disproportionately hurt by the influx of illegal labor.

Find out more about this Promise Kept by visiting PMPK2020.com

Promise #38
Give The Facts Plainly And Honestly—Keep Tweeting!

Donald Trump revolutionized American politics forever by using the social media platform Twitter to broadcast his message directly to the American people. As he explained in a tweet on December 30, 2017, "I use Social Media not because I like to, but because it is the only way to fight a VERY dishonest and unfair 'press,' now often referred to as Fake News Media. Phony and non-existent 'sources' are being used more often than ever. Many stories & reports a [*sic*] pure fiction."

Candidate Trump knew the fake news media would try to filter his message to make it unpalatable to the American people. His only recourse was to communicate directly to the people with no intermediary. That's not to say President Trump's administration has not been open to the press. Even many members of the press who don't agree with his policies have had to admit that Trump's White House has been more open than most recent administrations.

However, Trump has never stopped communicating to the people directly on Twitter, even when pressured by his advisors and others to stop. In the midst of the rigors of the presidency, he still makes time to use social media. President Trump's use of social media really is "modern day presidential." America needs a president willing to change with the technological tastes of the people. There are no ivory towers in the Trump White House.

Find out more about this Promise Kept by visiting PMPK2020.com

Promise #39
Grow The American Economy

Candidate Trump promised to use his savvy as a businessman to maximize the growth of the American economy. Politicians claimed for decades that they held the key to economic growth. The American people would put them in office only for stagnation to grip the nation. Another politician would come along and make the same empty promises, so the voters would give him a try only to get the same result. It was the true definition of insanity. When President Trump took office, everyone knew things were going to really change. Leftists were sure the economy would tank, while Trump voters believed as Phyllis Schlafly did that he was the "last best hope for America." Three solid years of growth should make clear who ended up being right. President Trump grew the American economy at a fantastic pace. Gross Domestic Product (GDP) growth went up, up, and up every quarter. GDP growth did go down in the first two quarters of 2020, but that was amid the COVID-19 pandemic. Few people believe GDP growth would have been possible under any administration. In fact, there is every reason to believe things would have been much worse had it not been for President Trump's early and decisive action to curb travel from the nation where the virus originated.

Looking at pre-COVID numbers and current recovery projections make it clear to see America's businessman president followed through on his pledge to grow the economy.

Find out more about this Promise Kept by visiting PMPK2020.com

Promise #40
Hire Americans First

Candidate Donald Trump's immigration platform proclaimed that he would make it the priority of the United States government to promote the hiring of American workers first. One might think something so elementary would have already been our national policy. But that was not the case. American employers have long used the H-1B visa program to import skilled laborers from nations like India rather than hiring ready and willing Americans. Phyllis Schlafly pointed out that, "Employers want aliens with H-1B visas not only because they can pay them less than U.S. technicians, but especially because the H-1B visas lock them into sticking with the sponsoring employer and prevent them from job-hopping for better pay as Americans do." Incentivizing American employers to hire non-Americans was our national policy until President Trump took office. True to his campaign pledge, he issued an executive order calling for companies to "Buy American, Hire American." This order limited the vast expanse of the H-1B system to incentivize the hiring of American, not foreign, workers for key jobs on American shores.

Not only was this another promise kept for President Trump, but it was a vital protection for new generations of American workers as well. College students with degrees in key STEM fields should have total assurance that our national policy is to reward their smart degree choices with a high-paying job and a bright future.

Find out more about this Promise Kept by visiting PMPK2020.com

Promise #41
Honor Hero Dog Conan At The White House

On October 27, 2019, an elite team of U.S. Army soldiers conducted a raid targeting the head of ISIS. The raid resulted in the death of Abu Bakr al-Baghdadi, who was the head of ISIS at the time. A heroic military dog named Conan was among the American contingent that took Baghdadi down. Conan chased him into a tunnel before the terrorist leader detonated a suicide vest. In the process, Conan was injured by exposure to live electrical wires. The next day, President Trump tweeted a declassified picture of Conan while praising him for his great work. Word of the dog's bravery spread rapidly, leading the Daily Wire to create a photoshopped image of President Trump giving Conan a medal. Trump retweeted the picture, promising that the real Conan would be honored at the White House soon. On November 25, President Trump kept his promise by holding a meeting with Conan at the White House. Trump called him a "tough cookie" and the "ultimate fighter."

By conducting this meeting, President Trump accomplished more than a photo op. He reminded the American people of the brave men and women (and dogs) who fight for freedom around the globe. Many soldiers conducting these daring raids are never honored because their identities must remain a secret. President Trump honored the incredible sacrifice of those elite soldiers right along with the hero dog Conan.

Find out more about this Promise Kept by visiting PMPK2020.com

Promise #42
If Manufacturers Leave There Will Be Consequences

Before President Trump came on the scene, there was no reason for American manufacturers to stay in America. As they saw it, patriotism doesn't pay the bills. Other countries could offer cheaper labor while not having to saddle them with the environmental and employment regulations so common here in America. Candidate Donald Trump promised that if American companies decide to forsake their American roots by moving manufacturing hubs overseas, there would be consequences for those failings. President Trump followed through with a perfect carrot-and-stick approach. He incentivized employers by cutting down on burdensome regulations. He also cut corporate taxes to make it all the more enticing for American businesses to stay American. However, while offering these great incentives, he implemented a system of tariffs to punish imports in certain key industries when American companies decide to move overseas.

Almost immediately, these business-friendly policies began bringing manufacturing back to America. Top companies like Apple, Boeing, Ford, Whirlpool, and GE brought thousands of jobs back to America. President Trump's proved that the U.S. can compete with the cheap labor in China, Mexico, and elsewhere. Many of these companies would like nothing more than to stay in America if only a smart businessman will help them from the Oval Office. President Trump mastered the art of both the carrot and the stick.

Find out more about this Promise Kept by visiting PMPK2020.com

Promise #43
Increase Government Transparency

One might think a president like Donald Trump would have closed off his White House to the press, only communicating to the outside world through his Twitter feed. While it is true that President Trump successfully mastered the art of using social media to spread his message to the American people, he is also one of the most transparent presidents in American history. He is the only president who has called the fake news media "the enemy of the people" while simultaneously opening himself and his administration up to the media's abuse like never before. In a way, Trump's transparency is the ultimate trolling of the media establishment he hates so much. The press are dying to say that President Trump is shutting them out and stifling their voice. Yet all they can do is cry about some name-calling. They cannot point to a single anti-media policy in the Trump White House. Even in liberal hit pieces aimed at destroying President Trump, reporters like the *Independent*'s David Usborne have to admit "Here's what's so confusing … This may, in fact, be the most transparent White House ever—and the most transparent President."

Usborne is right. People may not like what President Trump has to say, but almost no one thinks the President is hiding what he really thinks. The Trump administration is the transparent administration, just as he said it would be when he campaigned.

Find out more about this Promise Kept by visiting PMPK2020.com

Promise #44
Increase Oil Production

For decades, America was at the mercy of the tumultuous Middle Eastern nations in OPEC to get crude oil. The U.S. had to tiptoe around the whims of these governments because of the terrible bargaining power they held over the American people. Candidate Donald Trump knew what a powerful bargaining tool OPEC had over America, so he promised to revive the nation's languishing domestic oil production. He was able to make such a bold promise not only because of the need, but also because of America's vast natural resources. Plenty of oil waits beneath American soil just waiting to be extracted. Until the Trump administration, the federal government had been working against the oil industry by withholding oil-rich territory in vast unused public lands. Environmental regulators hindered oil industry development by stopping companies from using the highly effective "fracking" method to extract the oil. The science does not support rampant condemnation of fracking, but environmentalists saw it as an opportunity to stifle development, so they took it.

Clearly, President Trump had his work cut out for him, but he stepped up to the challenge right away. By September of 2018, America became the top oil producer in the world, surpassing other big oil producers like Russia and Saudi Arabia for the first time since 1973. The United States oil industry has a true industry ally in President Donald Trump.

Find out more about this Promise Kept by visiting PMPK2020.com

Promise #45
Keep Ford In The United States

When Ford Motor Company announced plans to invest $1.6 billion in a factory in Mexico, Donald Trump promised to keep Ford in the United States right along with other manufacturing giants. It didn't take long for Trump's promise to be fulfilled. In fact, Trump did not even have to step into the Oval Office for the spark to light. Ford announced a major change of plans on January 3rd, 2017, just before Trump took office. Not only did Ford decide not to build a giant factory in Mexico, but they also chose to reinvest that money on American soil by expanding their existing plant in Michigan to work on cutting-edge vehicular technology necessary for electric and autonomous cars.

America saw a similar phenomenon happening throughout the economy. The stock market did not wait to jump until President-elect Trump took office. Stocks went up immediately after his election because investors knew Trump was the more business-friendly candidate. Ford knew it could trust President Trump to make pro-business policy decisions to benefit everyone from CEOs to the guys on the production lines. The fact that Ford chose to invest in "green jobs" by developing electric cars is just icing on the cake. Trump managed to make a deal that benefitted manufacturers, employees, and environmentalists all at the same time! The mark of a true leader is being able to see business as more than a zero sum game.

Find out more about this Promise Kept by visiting PMPK2020.com

Promise #46
Keep Gitmo Open

President Trump knows how to speak in a way that resonates with the American people. He does not feel the need to speak in political platitudes. He just speaks his mind. That's what he did when he issued a key campaign promise during a speech in Las Vegas on February 24, 2016, saying, "Gitmo, we're keeping that open, and we're going to load it up with bad dudes. We're going to load it up with a lot of bad dudes out there." The detention facility at Guantánamo Bay in Cuba has been a political football for years now. President Barack Obama wanted to shut it down, but Congress consistently prevented him from doing it because they knew Americans didn't want hardened terrorists on their own shores. President Trump reversed course from the previous administration by issuing an executive order to keep the prison operational. Furthermore, he directed the Secretary of Defense to "re-examine our military detention policy" to ensure we were not releasing prisoners only to have to fight them again in the Middle East. Even the former head of ISIS was once released from American custody, only to go right back to murdering, pillaging, and raping.

Gitmo shouldn't be a political football. It should be a symbol of American strength. It should tell terrorists everywhere that America will punish those who threaten the lives of American citizens. "Bad dudes" beware.

Promise #47
Limit Legal Immigration

Illegal immigration is not the only kind of immigration candidate Donald Trump promised to address. He pledged to extend his America First attitude to legal immigration as well as illegal. He said that the policy of his administration would be to ensure that only the best and brightest from other nations would be coming to America. In accordance with this promise, he issued an executive order in August 2019 aimed at cutting down on the number of legal immigrants taking advantage of welfare programs. Specifically, the order said that green card or visa applicants would be denied if they were found to have taken social benefits like food stamps or housing vouchers for twelve out of the last thirty-six months.

Liberals decried this move as a targeted attempt to keep the poor people of other countries out of our nation. However, there is a big difference between poor people and those who cannot stand on their own two feet. The United States has no obligation to provide food stamps for the rest of the world. It's not that Americans are only willing to let multi-billionaires come to their nation. They just don't want people to come over if they cannot do so without drawing welfare. The American dream for which people come to America should not be the dream of living off of welfare and food stamps for the rest of their lives. America wants immigrants who relish the idea of making their own way in the land of opportunity.

Find out more about this Promise Kept by visiting PMPK2020.com

Promise #48
Lots More ICE Agents

Building a wall is by itself not enough to secure the southern border. Candidate Trump also promised to massively increase the number of agents employed by Immigration and Customs Enforcement (ICE) to remove illegal aliens. In the first days of his administration, he issued an executive order aimed at "Enhancing Public Safety in the Interior of the United States." In the order, he called for an increase of 10,000 immigration officers. This hiring blitz came at the very same time that President Trump directed his administration to enforce a hiring freeze on most other departments. As any good leader should, Trump reallocated resources to ensure national priorities were where they should be. He trimmed the fat of wasteful government bureaucracy and redirected that money to useful ends.

It's worth pointing out that the hiring of new immigration officers didn't stop at 10,000 as the initial order directed. In reality, the number of positions at the Department of Homeland Security increased by more than 21,000 in President Trump's first two years in office. That's a greater increase than in any other department during the Trump administration. Clearly, he knows where our nation's priorities lie. Nothing is more important than protecting the lives of American citizens from foreign threats, including violent criminal illegal aliens. Hiring more ICE agents is an investment into the safety of Americans nationwide.

Find out more about this Promise Kept by visiting PMPK2020.com

Promise #49
Lower Repatriation Tax For Businesses

Before President Trump took office, businesses were charged a 35% tax for bringing their money to America from overseas. This repatriation tax kept trillions of dollars from being invested in America's economy and citizenry. Donald Trump promised he would bring investment back home by dramatically cutting the repatriation tax. True to his word, Trump changed the tax law to allow companies to move cash to American soil for a dramatically reduced 15.5%. Other assets could be moved for only an 8% tax. Not only did this bold move cut the repatriation tax by more than half, but it was the first time the tax had been cut at all for 31 years. Americans were eager to see if Trump's bold move would pay off.

Sure enough, nearly half a trillion dollars were repatriated to the United States in the first half of 2018. Not only did that generate massive tax revenue for our federal government, but it also had the added advantage of providing an extra half trillion dollars of investment in the U.S. economy. That's the kind of masterful dealmaking America needs. Businesses get a much cheaper tax rate, the government gets more tax revenue, and the American economy gets a much-needed facelift. Everyone wins under the leadership of President Donald Trump. His policies give every American the tools they need to get a much better deal.

Promise #50
Make A Vote For Trump The Best You Ever Cast

It won't come as a surprise to anyone to read that President Trump is no stranger to making bold claims. He says what he thinks and he promises big. Yet, he is one of the few elected officials in America today with the commitment to follow through on his big promises. At a rally in Wilkes-Barre, Pennsylvania, he promised a crowd of thousands that he would make a vote for him "the best vote you have ever cast." The American people believed he would make their votes worth something, which is why they voted him into the highest office in the land.

Since that time, President Trump has done everything in his power to live up to that bold promise. When putting President Trump into the context of other presidential administrations, many have compared him to President Ronald Reagan. Yet, experts in the pro-life movement have openly said that the actions taken by Trump make him an even stronger advocate for life than Reagan was. Likewise, when the Heritage Foundation conducted a massive review of President Trump's first year in office, they concluded that he had accomplished more of his agenda than President Reagan had at that point in his presidency.

America has benefited from the courageous efforts of many fine presidents over the years, but President Trump has proven that a vote for him truly is the best vote anyone has cast in modern history.

Find out more about this Promise Kept by visiting PMPK2020.com

Promise #51
Work With The State Of Israel

The state of Israel is overwhelmingly supported by the American people. Israel stands as an island of democracy in a sea of theocratic authoritarianism. They are undoubtedly America's greatest strategic ally in the region. The people of Israel love America just as much as America loves them. However, America's goodwill is hampered by a highly partisan divide among national political figures. While Republican leaders and some Democrats stand by Israel, a growing minority of far-left Democrats call for America to totally divest from the Middle East's sole constitutional republic. Candidate Donald Trump promised to be a friend to the state of Israel. Of course, President Trump's signature show of support for the state of Israel was moving the American embassy to the Israeli capital of Jerusalem. However, it is also worth noting that President Trump's decision to tear up the Iran nuclear deal was met with great applause from the Israeli people. They knew the deal did nothing to prevent Iran from developing nuclear arms. In fact, the deal likely helped Iran reach that end by throwing billions of dollars their way. With Iranians being infamous for chanting "Death to Israel" in the streets, it is not hard to imagine who their first target might be.

While the Democrats distance themselves further and further from America's strategic and ideological ally in the Middle East, President Trump honors his commitment to support the state of Israel.

Find out more about this Promise Kept by visiting PMPK2020.com

Promise #52
Make Healthcare Prices More Transparent

America was built on the principles of free market economics where providers of goods and services compete for the business of consumers. This competition increases quality and reduces prices. However, some healthcare providers took advantage of the unique market share they held by hiding prices from consumers. That is why candidate Donald Trump promised to "require price transparency from all healthcare providers, especially doctors and healthcare organizations like clinics and hospitals." He went on to explain that "Individuals should be able to shop to find the best prices for procedures, exams, or any other medical-related procedure." The prevailing attitude of liberals is that America should amputate free market principles from healthcare because the system is broken. President Trump wisely recognized that just the opposite is true. There was not enough capitalism in the healthcare markets for tangible benefits to be realized. So he ordered his Department of Health and Human Services to require hospitals to make prices available online so consumers could shop around. He also worked to make insurance companies provide cost estimates for the services they cover.

Most Americans wouldn't go to a grocery store where prices were not clearly displayed on products. Why should anyone go to a hospital or insurance company that does the same thing? Thanks to President Trump, Americans don't have to.

Find out more about this Promise Kept by visiting PMPK2020.com

Promise #53
Make Japan Pay Its Fair Share For Military Protection

The United States maintains strategic military posts throughout the world, but particularly in Germany, Japan, and South Korea. Candidate Donald Trump voiced concern that these nations were not paying their fair share for the protection afforded them by the U.S. In a debate with Hillary Clinton, he said, "They do not pay us, but they should be paying us, because we are providing tremendous service and we're losing a fortune." Trump's comments resonated with the American people. After all, why should American leaders allow those nations to outperform us in manufacturing or innovation using the defense dollars that rightly belong in America? While in the presidency, Trump has put the nation's allies on notice that the terms of the agreements with them are going to change. Under another president, these threats might seem empty. However, with President Trump, he doesn't make threats lightly.

That is why it came as no surprise when he told Japan that he wants to increase their host nation support to $8 billion from the current $3.6 billion. Do not forget that their compensation does not just give them the security of American military forces on the ground, but the security of America's nuclear umbrella as well. The current deal with Japan expires in March 2021. Japan hopes Trump will lose his bid for reelection so they can continue taking America to the cleaners. Will we let them?

Find out more about this Promise Kept by visiting PMPK2020.com

Promise #54
Make Our Country Rich Again

An essential part of fulfilling America's vision of securing the right to the "pursuit of happiness" is giving even the poorest people the ability to achieve relative financial success. The role of the federal government is to facilitate a pro-business climate to empower entrepreneurship and innovation to thrive in a capitalist market. That might seem like a lot of technical policy jargon to some, but to those who want to create a better life for themselves and their families, it is everything. It should not be considered a coincidence that President Trump's pro-business policies have resulted in across-the-board prosperity to those who invest in the stock market. The day after President Trump won the 2016 presidential election, the S&P 500 stood just shy of 2,100 points. In 2017, the S&P 500 reached 62 all-time highs. The trend continued with 18 all-time highs in 2018 and 19 in 2019. When the market peaked on February 19, 2020, it stood at an unprecedented 3,386 points.

Of course, the market went down considerably with COVID-19, but the mainstream media won't tell you that even at its worst point in the COVID crisis, the S&P still closed higher than it was before Trump won in 2016. The market has rapidly recovered since that time. President Trump is following through on his promise to make our country rich again.

Promise #55
Make Our NATO Allies Pay Their Fair Share

Candidate Donald Trump summed up his position on NATO very succinctly at a speech in Miami. "I think NATO's great, but it's got to be modernized, and countries that we're protecting have to pay what they're supposed to be paying." Even NATO's commander under the Obama administration agreed, pointing out that only five of twenty-eight NATO members met their pledged spending on defense. Only three nations met their goal of spending twenty percent of that defense money on major weapons systems. While the U.S., the U.K., and Poland followed through, the rest of the alliance let Russia get ahead. Following through on his promise, President Trump put incredible pressure on the member nations of NATO to carry out their own commitments. He pointed out how America pays for sixty-nine percent of defense spending despite the fact that the U.S. economy comprises less than half of NATO's economy overall.

Trump's pressure is leading to real results. For the fourth year in a row, NATO's defense spending has increased. Seven member nations have now met their commitments, with sixteen nations unveiling plans to reach their commitments over time. America just needed a leader who was willing to stand up to other nations and give a voice to the American people. As NATO's largest contributor, Americans have a right to voice their concerns when other nations aren't pitching in. President Trump is making it happen.

Find out more about this Promise Kept by visiting PMPK2020.com

Promise #56
Make The "Brand" Of America Great Again

Candidate Donald Trump struck a chord when he promised to make the "brand" of America great again. Americans were tired of politically correct politicians going on "apology tours" around the world badmouthing their own nation just because of the politically correct American left. Patriots wanted a president who was unapologetically pro-America, who believes America is the greatest nation on the face of the Earth, and who would act accordingly. Patriots found that president in Donald Trump. Under President Trump, America hasn't been the world's policeman or the world's punching bag. Unless someone is openly hostile to America they have largely been left alone. The principle of America First means looking after American affairs rather than entangling the nation in the affairs of others. That does not mean Americans roll over when their interests are threatened abroad. Whether someone attacks from the streets of Raqqa or the halls of the United Nations, Trump's administration responds promptly and decisively.

The apology tours are over with the Trump administration. He has made it clear that America is not ashamed to put American citizens first. The American people proudly stand beside freedom-loving people throughout the globe, but protecting the rights of American citizens always comes first. President Trump promised to make the brand of America great again, and that is exactly what he is doing.

Find out more about this Promise Kept by visiting PMPK2020.com

Promise #57
Move U.S. Embassy To Jerusalem

Every political candidate makes big promises, but so few of them actually follow through. Moving the U.S. embassy to Jerusalem is a prime example of this. Presidential candidates of both parties have been promising to make the move since Richard Nixon, but no one had the boldness to do it until President Trump. He promised the American Israel Public Affairs Committee, "We will move the American embassy to the eternal capital of the Jewish people, Jerusalem." That's exactly what he did. The lengthy saga of the embassy move has been a titanic struggle between bureaucratic nonsense and common sense. Anti-Israel paper-pushers at the State Department and leftist television pundits fought tooth and nail to keep the embassy in Tel Aviv. Their one and only argument was that moving the embassy would make Muslims mad at the U.S., triggering a cataclysmic war in the Middle East. Nothing of the kind actually happened. The embassy move strengthened the nation's relations with Israel and the Jewish people.

Making the move should have been an elementary decision. Israel has claimed Jerusalem as their capital city since 1980. Their prime minister, parliament, and high court are all housed in Jerusalem. Not to put the American embassy in Jerusalem was an affront to America's strongest ally in the region. Despite all this, only President Donald Trump had the boldness to ignore the State Department bureaucrats and follow through on his promise.

Find out more about this Promise Kept by visiting PMPK2020.com

Promise #58
Neutralize Defense Sequestration

Never one to mince words, candidate Donald Trump promised to "build a military that's gonna be much stronger than it is right now. It's gonna be so strong, nobody's going to mess with us." An essential part of carrying this out was eliminating defense sequestration. Sequestration, which military leaders called the "biggest challenge to the military's readiness," came with the Budget Control Act of 2011. In it, the Department of Defense receives an automatic funding cut whenever Congress and the White House do not make certain other cuts in the national budget. As a result, the nation's military has been terribly under-funded for nearly a decade.

For fiscal year 2020, President Trump negotiated a budget deal with Democrat leaders to give the military a 3% increase in funding, for a total of $738 billion. Trump called it "a real compromise in order to give another big victory to our Great Military and Vets!" Obviously, this is not just a win for the military. This is a win for all Americans. After all, if Americans cannot defend their nation and their interests against foreign military aggression, none of the rest of the budget matters. Total military superiority is totally essential. The people of America can all sleep safely at night knowing that the nation's military is ready to tackle any threat thanks to this great new deal negotiated by President Trump.

Promise #59
Never Be In A Bicycle Race

We all remember the iconic moment when Donald Trump announced his candidacy for the presidency. We all remember his commitment to build the wall, his pledge to put Americans first, and his creed to make America great again. However, what few people remember from this iconic scene in American history is Trump's promise to never participate in a bicycle race. While the promise itself is admittedly comical, the context of the promise is very serious. Trump was pointing out how Secretary of State John Kerry seemed to care more about his cycling hobby than protecting the American people. Indeed, he broke his leg while participating in a bicycle race in the middle of a four-stop trip to Europe on behalf of the American people. Due to his broken leg, he canceled plans to participate in an international conference aimed at addressing the threat of ISIS. In a lot of ways, Trump's "no bicycle race" promise was a metaphor for his commitment to put the American people first in international negotiations. No longer would the needs of our own people play second fiddle to the whims of career bureaucrats with nothing better to do than ride their bicycles.

Whether you take the promise literally or figuratively, the fact remains that President Trump has yet to break it. President Trump puts the American people first, and there are no reports indicating that the president has participated in a bicycle race.

Find out more about this Promise Kept by visiting PMPK2020.com

Promise #60
Never Ever Stop Fighting

Candidate Donald Trump promised to never stop fighting for the American people. If any president deserves a break from fighting, it would be President Trump. He has withstood constant opposition from all sides from the moment he announced his candidacy. The traditional "honeymoon period" afforded to so many other presidential administrations was never given to Trump. As soon as he took office, he was lambasted by attempts to invalidate the election, followed by the bogus Mueller witch hunts and the equally bogus impeachment coup. Despite all this, President Trump never stopped fighting for the American people. In fact, he has not even slowed down. Knowing full well that every promise kept would only result in more outrage from the Left, Trump fights on to carry out what he promised to do. Attempts to invalidate the election fizzled out when the American people realized that their will should not be ignored. The Mueller witch hunt fell apart because there was no collusion to prosecute, despite the millions of taxpayer dollars spent to find it. The impeachment coup fell flat because President Trump refused to let the American people lose their champion to ridiculous made-up charges.

In the midst of all this, President Trump fought on. The only thing more admirable than President Trump's fighting spirit is the fact that he fights for We The People. He is a fighter by nature, a fighter who loves America more than anything else.

Find out more about this Promise Kept by visiting PMPK2020.com

Promise #61
Nobody Will Be Pushing Us Around

Candidate Donald Trump campaigned on the vision of restored American strength abroad as well as at home. He laid out his plans to rebuild America's military to face the threats of today while proclaiming to the world America's commitment to defend our interests. As Trump put it, "Nobody will be pushing us around." With a bold commitment like that, it is no wonder the American people voted to give President Donald Trump the chance to carry out his vision. Dictators quickly rose to challenge President Trump on this commitment. Particularly, North Korean dictator Kim Jong Un flexed his flabby muscles by testing intercontinental ballistic missiles allegedly capable of reaching American shores. On top of that, he began hurling insults at President Trump over Twitter.

President Trump wisely chose to confront this madman directly. He called Kim out, while also extending an olive branch. No matter how high the pressure got, Trump never backed down. Upon realizing threats and intimidation would not work, Kim Jong Un turned to a diplomatic approach. Before long, Trump became the first American head of state to meet with a member of the Kim family. Trump even historically stepped onto North Korean soil with Kim. Clearly, President Trump's policy of not letting anyone push us around has proven highly successful when dealing with foreign bullies who threaten American safety and security.

Find out more about this Promise Kept by visiting PMPK2020.com

Promise #62
Nominate Pro-Life Justices

A pivotal part of Donald Trump's 2016 presidential campaign was pointing out the clear differences between himself and Hillary Clinton. He understood that he could separate himself from Hillary by pointing out his commitment to nominating pro-life justices to the United States Supreme Court as well as to the lower federal courts. Americans knew that they could expect nothing but judicial activist judges from the likes of Hillary Clinton. Trump contrasted by saying, "The justices that I'm going to appoint will be pro-life. They will have a conservative bent." In a nation still hurting from devastating Supreme Court decisions like *Roe v. Wade*, that promise helped propel Trump into the Oval Office.

The abortion issue is particularly important when connected to the Supreme Court because so many good pro-life laws are struck down by judges. The nation is becoming increasingly pro-life, so true representatives of the people are increasingly voting to defend the rights of the unborn. Consequently, pro-abortion activists are having to turn to the courts to force their views on everyone else. President Trump saw the heightened importance of this issue, which is why he made it a priority to secure Supreme Court justices and federal judges who claim strong pro-life views. Judges may not be elected by the people, but President Donald Trump most certainly was. He is a true champion of the pro-life movement where it matters most.

Find out more about this Promise Kept by visiting PMPK2020.com

Promise #63
Not Be Controlled By Lobbyists

One might say that lobbyists and special interest groups are a dime a dozen in Washington, D.C., but there is a lot more cash involved than that. Every year, countless elected officials on every level are bought and paid for by lobbyists. It's amazing what a well-placed campaign contribution can buy these days. Candidate Donald Trump promised that he would work for his actual employers -the American people- rather than catering to the lobbyists and special interests.

As proof of this, Donald Trump largely self-funded his 2016 campaign for the presidency. He cut out the massive donations from special interests that so often plague the Establishment. In total, he personally contributed $66.1 million to his own campaign. He had initially claimed he would spend $100 million, but he ended up being more efficient than even he thought. What campaign money he did take in from outside sources was from average American men and women who saw the vision he cast for America's future and wanted to be a part of it. In the critical final stretch leading up Election Day, 74% of contributions to his campaign were coming from small donors. Clearly, Donald Trump was no puppet of the Establishment elites.

In the presidency, Trump lives out the independence he had shown on the campaign trail. He works only for We The People because he truly loves America. He cannot be bought.

Find out more about this Promise Kept by visiting PMPK2020.com

Promise #64
Only Let In Immigrants Who Love Americans

Contrary to what the mainstream media would have Americans to believe, Donald Trump did not campaign on a platform of hatred for anyone, including immigrants. That kind of dangerous caricature is exactly why the American people do not trust the mainstream media anymore. In reality, Trump said he wanted to restrict immigration to only those immigrants who love America. There is a reason the media did not want to report it that way. They know the vast majority of Americans agree with what Trump actually said. After all, who is publicly advocating for America to harbor the people who hate her? Unfortunately, even though common sense should dictate that the government keep people out if they hate America, the nation's immigration policies were woefully inadequate for the task.

Following through with his promise, President Trump made significant reform to the way the nation takes in immigrants. He instituted a hold on immigration from select nations that are well-known for their terrorist ties. He changed the refugee system to make sure anyone who comes here claiming asylum is someone who will embrace the American way of life. There is still much more to be done, but President Trump is taking real concrete steps to ensure that the immigrants welcomed into the land of opportunity are ones whose hearts truly burn to embrace her culture, heritage, and constitutional form of government.

Find out more about this Promise Kept by visiting PMPK2020.com

Promise #65
Pick Judges Who Support Second Amendment

The United States Supreme Court holds tremendous sway over every aspect of government, including the way in which the Bill of Rights is upheld throughout the nation. That is why candidate Donald Trump clearly made the case for choosing judges who will uphold Second Amendment protections on bearing arms. In his October 2016 debate against Hillary Clinton, Trump said, "We need a Supreme Court that in my opinion is going to uphold the Second Amendment, and all amendments, but the Second Amendment, which is under absolute siege." As soon as he stepped into the Oval Office, he had to fill the vacancy left by the late Justice Antonin Scalia. He filled it with conservative Justice Neil Gorsuch. It did not take long before Trump's promise of picking pro-Second Amendment judges was put to the test. The High Court took on its first Second Amendment case in a decade shortly after Gorsuch was put on the Court. The case *New York State Rifle & Pistol Association Inc. v. City of New York* dealt with the constitutionality of one of the city's burdensome gun control laws.

The High Court ended up declaring the case moot because the city changed the law in question, but Justice Gorsuch joined Justices Alito and Thomas in dissenting the ruling, saying that the city's unconstitutional conduct deserved to be addressed. Justice Gorsuch's actions prove President Trump's dedication to honoring his commitment to pro-Second Amendment judges on the Supreme Court.

Find out more about this Promise Kept by visiting PMPK2020.com

Promise #66
Pick Judges Who Uphold The Constitution

Candidate Donald Trump promised "to appoint justices to the United States Supreme Court who will uphold our laws and our Constitution." His declaration was met with vigorous cheering and applause from the packed crowd of patriotic RNC delegates from throughout the nation who filled the stands of the Rocket Mortgage FieldHouse in Cleveland, Ohio. When Trump made that promise, he was decrying what Phyllis Schlafly called "judicial supremacy." That term refers to a judge who believes his personal political beliefs are more important than the Constitution. Judicial supremacists issue rulings based on what they think the law should be, rather than on what the plain text of the U.S. Constitution dictates.

These kinds of judges who legislate from the bench lack a basic understanding of how our republic is supposed to work. Any elementary school student can tell you that the Legislative Branch is supposed to make the laws, the Executive Branch is supposed to enforce the laws, and the Judicial Branch is supposed to interpret the laws. If the courts do not like it, they should step down and run for Congress. As a candidate, Donald Trump promised to pick Supreme Court judges who recognize the basic differences of the branches. He has followed through on that by nominating Justices Gorsuch and Kavanaugh to the Supreme Court. Trump selected the barristers he knew were the most likely to be true champions of the Constitution.

Find out more about this Promise Kept by visiting PMPK2020.com

Promise #67
Pick Someone From His List To Replace Justice Scalia

Candidate Donald Trump made it clear that he fully intended to pick a Supreme Court justice who would follow in the groundbreaking footsteps of the conservative titan Justice Antonin Scalia. To clarify Trump's position on selecting good judges, he released a list of twenty-one judges he would consider when filling the vacancy left by the late Antonin Scalia. Even before his election, Trump pledged to pick a judge from off of that list. Any American could investigate the judges for themselves to determine if the kind of scholars Trump was looking at were truly a good fit for Scalia's seat.

Just as Trump promised, Neil Gorsuch came off of that list. In late 2017, President Trump updated the list with five more names. One of those names was Brett Kavanaugh, who went on to be Trump's next appointee. Liberals like to act as though everything President Trump does is totally unpredictable, but there was nothing unpredictable about Trump's actions. He made a list of solid constitutional judges, shared that list with the American people, and nominated one of the judges for the open position. President Donald Trump stuck by his nominees despite the terrible vitriol spewed by the Democrats. Picking a name from a pre-released list may not make for dramatic news coverage, but it shows the seriousness of President Trump's dedication to standing by the promises he made during the campaign.

Find out more about this Promise Kept by visiting PMPK2020.com

Promise #68
Place Lifetime Ban On White House Officials Lobbying For Foreign Governments

Let's be honest. Even if you are a great White House official, you still only have a maximum of eight years in a particular presidential administration. An eight-year cap on your career path is not appealing to most people. As a result, many White House officials in previous administrations have gone on to become lobbyists to capitalize on their connections in the government. Sometimes, they have even lobbied on behalf of foreign governments.

This career path creates a dangerous conflict of interest. After all, if you know you will be in the White House for eight years, then go on to make twice as much money for a foreign government for twenty years, you are going to be beholden to that future employer. Even while you are in the White House, you will be looking out for the interests of a foreign government to make sure your future position is secure.

As Donald Trump ran on the theme of draining the Swamp, he promised to institute "a lifetime ban on White House officials lobbying on behalf of a foreign government." He made it clear that everyone working on his team had to be playing to win for America. When President Trump took office in 2017, he immediately signed an executive order accomplishing this very goal. President Trump made sure that the officials in his White House work only for We the People.

Find out more about this Promise Kept by visiting PMPK2020.com

Promise #69
The Powerful Won't Beat Up On People Who Cannot Defend Themselves

A major theme of Donald Trump's 2016 presidential campaign was standing up for the people who cannot stand up for themselves. We see this any time someone goes up against the federal government. If some bureaucrat does not like you and "accidentally" places you on the FBI's list of people who cannot purchase firearms, what can you do? If a paper-pusher tries to keep your conservative nonprofit from getting 501(c)3 status, what are your options? Maybe you could sue the federal government, but they are armed with a legion of lawyers and a mountain of taxpayer dollars. For most of us, fighting that fight is not feasible. We need an elected leader who will look out for our interests.

Donald Trump promised to be different. He promised to intervene when Deep Staters pick on ordinary Americans. Since taking office, he has worked to give new avenues for the American people to petition their government for the redress of grievances. Most notably, he set up a hotline for veterans to file complaints against the Department of Veterans Affairs. By staying tuned to social media, President Trump has an unprecedented source of communication with average citizens. The American people have a champion in President Donald Trump. He still has more of the Swamp left to drain, but we can rest assured knowing that we have someone who will fight the Swamp on our behalf.

Find out more about this Promise Kept by visiting PMPK2020.com

Promise #70
Prioritize Mental Health Care

Candidate Donald Trump's 2016 platform on healthcare reform called for action to prioritize mental health care for the American people. As he puts it, "Families, without the ability to get the information needed to help those who are ailing, are often not given the tools to help their loved ones." Particularly in light of the growing trend of horrendous mass shootings plaguing our schools, targeted mental health reforms are essential. That is why President Trump responded to the shooting at Stoneman Douglas High School by giving mental healthcare particular emphasis in his 2020 budget proposal. In total, he proposed designating $133 million in targeted training for school employees to better understand the symptoms of mental illness so they can work with parents to give troubled youth the help they need before it's too late. In addition, he proposed an impressive $13 million increase in funding for community mental health services block grants.

For far too many decades, politicians have thrown around the problem of our ailing mental health industry without actually doing something about it. This tends to be one of those oft repeated campaign promises that are never fulfilled by either party. Mental health care is a big issue that deserves real attention and action. President Trump has begun taking the small steps necessary to make a big change in the way our nation perceives and treats mental illness.

Promise #71
Protect All Kids Equally

The proverbial practice of "baby kissing" is a common trope about campaigning politicians. The idea is that candidates can curry favor among voters by appearing to care about the needs of their children and grandchildren. For that reason, it is unlikely anyone batted an eye when candidate Donald Trump promised to protect the interests of children in his administration. He may not have been the first candidate to do so, but what sets Trump apart is his wife's unprecedented efforts to address the biggest contemporary problems faced by our children today. First Lady Melania Trump developed her "Be Best" campaign as a three-pillared effort. The first pillar addresses general well-being as the foundation of facing modern problems. She calls for children to be taught to "carry on Americans' legacy of compassion, service, and patriotism." The second pillar of "Be Best" addresses the issue of online safety. Today's youth face problems online never experienced by previous generations. It is important to teach them to prevent cyberbullying and avoid dangerous interactions with strangers. The third pillar addresses the growing opioid epidemic, particularly among pregnant women. Curbing opioid abuse is a key component in protecting the next generation from prenatal harm.

The Trump administration does not stop at giving lip service to the needs of children. President Trump and his wife Melania are tackling the modern problems threatening every American child.

Find out more about this Promise Kept by visiting PMPK2020.com

Promise #72
Protect American Intellectual Property

Intellectual property may not be the most widely discussed topic on the political scene, but it is certainly one of the most important. America's meteoric rise to become the world's biggest superpower is a direct result of the innovation which characterized the American Industrial Revolution. You probably heard about the Industrial Revolution in school, but your teacher likely did not tell you what caused it. Article 1 Section 8 of the U.S. Constitution gives Congress the power to "promote the progress of science and useful arts, by securing for limited times to authors and inventors the exclusive right to their respective writings and discoveries." This exclusive right, which came in the form of our patent and trademark system, resulted in a strong financial incentive for American inventors.

Unfortunately, China has been abusing American innovation for decades by not honoring our patents. Candidate Trump promised that "If China does not stop its illegal activities, including its theft of American trade secrets and intellectual property, I will apply countervailing duties until China ceases and desists." The President opened trade negotiations with China in 2019 and imposed high tariffs on Chinese goods. President Trump followed through on this campaign promise because American intellectual property is an important American asset. An action to protect the American inventor is an action to protect America's great economic engine.

Find out more about this Promise Kept by visiting PMPK2020.com

Promise #73
Protect Religious Freedom

The right to freely express one's religion is found in the First Amendment to our Constitution for a reason. Millions of Americans consider the free expression of their faith to be a fundamental right given to them by God. We want elected officials to respect the preeminence of this right by securing it in policies favorable to religious expression. President Obama waged an eight-year war against our Judeo Christian heritage and America was ready for a change. Speaking at a closed-door meeting with religious leaders, candidate Trump promised to fiercely defend religious freedom. Since taking office, President Trump has consistently made respect of religion a hallmark of his administration. He quickly signed an executive order in 2017 reversing course on the practice of attacking religious institutions engaged in political action. In 2018, he established the White House Faith and Opportunity Initiative to give faith leaders an important voice in the Executive Branch. In 2020, he signed another executive order advancing international religious freedom. From the earliest days of COVID-19, Trump's Justice Department stood with churches who were unfairly targeted by burdensome restrictions.

President Trump is a tireless defender of religious freedom. Donald Trump has consistently made it clear that the culture of his administration will be favorable to the free exercise of religious faith.

Find out more about this Promise Kept by visiting PMPK2020.com

Promise #74
Pull Out Of Iran Deal

Donald Trump's promise to tear up the Iran nuclear deal was another hallmark of his presidential campaign. As the author of *The Art of the Deal*, Trump was uniquely situated to criticize the bad deal President Obama had forced on the American people. We were all told that the deal was supposed to prevent the dangerous Iranian regime from developing nuclear weapons. In reality, the deal gave Iran a giant pile of cash valued at over $50 billion, plus other assets conservatively estimated between $50 and $70 billion. On top of that, key sanctions against Iran were lifted. In return, Iran pinky promised not to build nuclear weapons, but refuses to accept the monitoring necessary to verify that they are actually holding up their end of the bargain.

With terms like that, it is no wonder Donald Trump saw this as a bad deal for the American people. The last thing we need is a nuclear Iran. That is why he came through on his promise to tear up the deal on May 8, 2018. President Obama may have liked the idea of including a deal with Iran on his presidential legacy checklist, but his ego should not preempt the safety of the American people. Thankfully, President Trump prioritizes keeping promises above building out his own legacy. Just like President Trump said when he announced the withdrawal from the deal, "When I make promises, I keep them."

Promise #75
Put Americans First

There are lots of reasons someone might want to be the president. Some might want the financial benefits. Some might crave the power. Some might want the attention. Donald Trump needed none of that. He was already rich and powerful. He already had the attention of the entire nation with his career in television. He certainly did not do it to make friends with famous people. Many of those people used to be his friends before he took office, but have abandoned him as he puts We The People first. In the end, it all comes down to one simple fact. Donald Trump took on the presidency because he loves America. He campaigned on putting Americans first, and that is precisely what he has done. He is not beholden to special interests, lobbyists, or foreign governments. His immigration policies protect American lives from violent gangs. His trade deals protect American manufacturing from foreign job-stealing. His tax cuts protect American families from burdensome financial interference.

A commitment to serve We The People may sound like a gimmicky campaign trick, but President Trump has demonstrated that commitment time and again. His quest to put Americans first permeates every corner of his administration. When you compare his four-year track record to the track record of any career politician who has lived on taxpayer dime for decades, there is no question who is truly committed to putting Americans first.

Find out more about this Promise Kept by visiting PMPK2020.com

Promise #76
Quickly Defeat ISIS

As the Islamic State swept across the Middle East, Americans were understandably worried. The terrorists had already proven themselves capable of executing terrible acts of violence and destruction far outside their region. How much more could the American people expect when the radical Islamic terrorists controlled enough territory to hold ten million souls captive? At the time, the U.S. had a president who was unwilling to even say the words "radical Islamic terrorism," much less defeat them. That is why Donald Trump issued a solemn promise to the American people that he would quickly defeat ISIS and bring an end to their reign of terror. Less than a year into President Trump's administration, he accomplished this monumental goal. From June 6 through October 17 of 2017, Syrian Democratic Forces (SDF) fought bravely to seize the ISIS capital of Raqqa. To make that siege possible, the U.S. led a coalition to perform 4,450 critical airstrikes. America also supported the battle with 500 special forces operatives, heavy weapons, intelligence, and communications support.

The SDF was able to fight with the knowledge that they were backed by our unsurpassed might. Gone were the days when America timidly refused to engage with international bullies. President Trump put the world on watch. He made it clear that the United States of America will meet any aggressor who threatens American lives with overwhelming military might.

Find out more about this Promise Kept by visiting PMPK2020.com

Promise #77
Renegotiate NAFTA

The North American Free Trade Agreement was signed by President Bill Clinton in 1993 and took effect in 1994. Clinton promised that NAFTA would lead to "more exports and more jobs for the United States." Instead, we were given an annual trade deficit. After just two decades of NAFTA, imports from Mexico went up by 500%. That led to an increase in illegal drugs too. On top of that, Mexican truckers were allowed to carry their loads deep inside the continental U.S. despite the fact that neither their trucks nor their drivers licenses were approved for use in America. Donald Trump promised to "Modernize NAFTA into a 21st Century trade agreement." As President, Trump set about to accomplish his goal by negotiating USMCA, which is an acronym for the United States-Mexico-Canada Agreement. In this new agreement, not only were many of the shortcomings of NAFTA addressed, but smart modernizations were also implemented to tackle trade issues specific to the 21st Century. Notably, USMCA includes robust protection of intellectual property and digital trade, which is not even mentioned in the NAFTA negotiated in the 1990s.

Whether anyone supported NAFTA when it was implemented, anyone can see that it was woefully out of date. President Trump wisely brought Mexico and Canada to the negotiating table so he could secure smart deals for the benefit of the American people. Renegotiating NAFTA was a critical part of his successful deal-making strategy.

Find out more about this Promise Kept by visiting PMPK2020.com

Promise #78
Repeal Obama's Greenhouse Gas Emissions Executive Order

President Barack Obama issued an executive order in 2015 to force the federal government to embrace the environmentalist agenda. He demanded a dramatic reduction in greenhouse gas emissions while increasing reliance on renewable energy. In a perfect world, that might not be a bad thing. However, the biggest problem of federal politicians is that they think the federal bureaucracy exists in an imaginary perfect world. In reality, they need to stick to a budget just like anyone else. Renewable energy technology simply has not advanced to the point where it can viably produce 30% of the federal government's energy. Our current electrical grid relies on around 20% renewables nationwide. However, some areas use much less than that because they simply do not have the right conditions for solar, wind, or hydroelectric power generation. The federal government has offices all over the nation. We cannot simply rely on wind power from DC's endless supply of hot air.

President Trump repealed this executive order with one of his own. He instructed all federal departments to follow the energy regulations set forth by Congress to protect the environment, while simultaneously striving to reduce waste and cut costs. That's the kind of budget-conscious administration we need. Renewable energy is fine, but we shouldn't set arbitrary deadlines at exorbitant taxpayer expense.

Find out more about this Promise Kept by visiting PMPK2020.com

Promise #79
Repeal Obamacare Individual Mandate

Much of the 2010 Tea Party wave came as a result of Obamacare's overreaching federal interference. In fact, the "Tea" in Tea Party is an acronym for "Taxed Enough Already." One particularly egregious tax came in the form of the Obamacare individual mandate that required all Americans to have health insurance approved by the federal government. If someone chose not to spend their money on health insurance, they were hit by a stiff $695 penalty. Donald Trump promised to repeal this burdensome mandate. After all, the tax was aimed squarely at Americans who could not afford health insurance, mainly those making less than $50,000 annually. Why would anyone want to charge those people an extra $1,390 per married couple? That is insane.

President Trump stopped the insanity by repealing the individual mandate via the Tax Cuts and Jobs Act of 2017. Democrats complained this would result in Americans not having health insurance, but they miss the point. The federal government has no business telling you what to buy with your hard-earned money. If you want to spend the money on health insurance, you should have that option. However, if you don't want to spend money on health insurance, if you cannot afford health insurance, or if you want coverage that does not meet the government's standard, you should not be saddled with a huge tax. President Trump delivered.

Find out more about this Promise Kept by visiting PMPK2020.com

Promise #80
Repealing Net Neutrality

Net neutrality may sound great in theory, but the name can be deceiving. Just like the Affordable Care Act was neither affordable nor did it provide care, and just like free trade is not really free, so too is net neutrality far from neutral. In reality, we all know there are a few large tech companies accounting for a significant percentage of the traffic online. Companies like Google, Facebook, and Twitter take up much more of the internet than a lot of other sites. However, these companies do not want to pay their fair share for the space they take up. So, they invented "net neutrality" to give themselves a financial advantage. It is no wonder President Trump called net neutrality a "top-down power grab" and promised to get rid of it. On June 11, 2018, President Trump's Federal Communications Commission followed through by issuing a full repeal of net neutrality rules. In its place, FCC chairman Ajit Pai instituted the Restoring Internet Freedom Order, which empowered the Federal Trade Commission to "police internet service providers for anticompetitive acts and unfair or deceptive practices."

Big Tech companies may want "neutrality" when it benefits them, but they certainly do not support neutrality when it comes to conservative viewpoints on their platforms. President Trump was right to roll back phony net neutrality so Big Tech does not get a special break at the expense of the rest of us.

Find out more about this Promise Kept by visiting PMPK2020.com

Promise #81
Free Americans Imprisoned Abroad

The common phrase "out of sight, out of mind" can easily take a very deadly twist when it comes to Americans imprisoned abroad. Whether the imprisonment comes at the hands of a hostile government or a rogue terrorist group, the president of the United States plays an important role in ensuring that all American citizens come home safely. However, presidents in recent years have dropped the ball on this pivotal duty. That's why candidate Donald Trump promised to take his job seriously. He tweeted on October 23, 2016, "Well, Iran has done it again. Taken two of our people and asking for a fortune for their release. This doesn't happen if I'm president!" President Trump did not forget this important promise. As our nation's chief dealmaker, he has boldly worked on behalf of imprisoned Americans to secure their prompt release. Under President Trump's direction, the missionary Joshua Holt was released from Venezuela. American pastor Andrew Brunson was released from Turkey after President Trump called out Turkey's president on Twitter. Michael White was released from Iran. Sam Goodwin was released from Syria. Three more were released from North Korea. The list goes on and on.

America needs a president with the boldness to take on the largest hostile governments and the compassion to care for the plight of even one American held unjustly overseas. President Donald Trump has proven himself to be such a president.

Find out more about this Promise Kept by visiting PMPK2020.com

Promise #82
Require Two Regulations Cut For Every One New Federal Regulation

Federal regulation is the bane of freedom-loving Americans everywhere. There is burdensome federal intrusion in just about every facet of American life. Want to sell milk from your own cows to your neighbor? There's a regulation for that. Onion rings at your new restaurant? Here's a side order of regulation. Free a whale tangled in your fishing nets? Believe it or not, there's a regulation for that too. Want to own a vending machine? You guessed it: more federal regulation. Candidate Donald Trump promised to cut down on the number of burdensome federal regulations crushing American business owners, property owners, and others. In fact, he issued a very specific promise to cut two old regulations for every one new regulation introduced. And he completely blew this promise out of the water! In the autumn 2018 edition of the semiannual Unified Agenda of Federal Regulatory and Deregulatory Actions, the administration revealed that they had wiped out a whopping sixteen regulations for every new regulation added. That means less federal bureaucracy, more freedom, and more opportunity for American businesses.

If President Trump were truly the power-hungry tyrant the mainstream media make him out to be, wouldn't he be indiscriminately adding arbitrary rules to exercise his own power? Instead, he's cutting back federal power to return it to the states and the American people.

Find out more about this Promise Kept by visiting PMPK2020.com

Promise #83
Restore Law And Order

President Obama had the chance to unite Americans like no other president before. Yet, instead of bringing people together, he chose to drive people apart. As the nation's top law enforcement officer, he turned people away from trusting the very law enforcement officers sworn to serve and protect them. President Trump promised to be the law and order president and support those who protect us every day.

Donald Trump consistently voices his support for law enforcement, but his support goes far beyond mere words. In August 2017, the Department of Justice announced a plan to reverse an old Obama policy preventing local law enforcement agencies from obtaining surplus military gear. Leftists like to throw around the term "militarized police force" as a dirty word, but have you seen what the criminals look like these days? Rioters use shields, lasers, and explosives to assault the police. They set fires to buildings and endanger the officers as well as innocent civilians. Giving local law enforcement access to lifesaving gear only makes sense. In the midst of the riots, President Trump has done nothing but offer support to mayors and governors throughout the nation. Leaders in Democrat-controlled enclaves are often too embarrassed to accept the President's generous offer. However, President Trump's constant offer of support to municipalities in the name of law and order is still a significant improvement from previous administrations.

Find out more about this Promise Kept by visiting PMPK2020.com

Promise #84
Reverse Obama's Executive Action On Gun Control

As President Obama was on his way out the door, he instituted a rule striping tens of thousands of Americans of their Constitutional right to bear arms. He made this rule change through executive action, not through an act of Congress. It is easy to see why. Congress never would have supported the outlandish action Obama took. He deceptively claimed the rule was supposed to keep mentally ill people from owning firearms. I do not know anyone who wants actually unstable and dangerous people to have guns. However, Obama's claim is way off base. He included people with eating disorders and anxiety right along with the seriously mentally impaired. The president has no business unilaterally taking away Second Amendment rights with no due process just because someone has an eating disorder. It would take guns away from law abiding citizens, and it would discourage people with eating disorders from getting the help they need.

At a rally in Biloxi, Mississippi, Trump said, "The system's supposed to be you get the Democrats, you get the Republicans, and you make deals. [Obama] can't do that. ... He's going to sign another executive order having to do with the Second Amendment. ... I will veto. I will unsign that so fast." Like he promised, President Trump justifiably nullified Obama's egregious overreaching gun grab. Interestingly, he did not have to use executive action like Obama did. Instead, he signed H.J. Res. 40, which received bipartisan support in Congress.

Find out more about this Promise Kept by visiting PMPK2020.com

Promise #85
Revive American Manufacturing

Donald Trump became the first Republican presidential candidate to win in Michigan since 1988. The manufacturing hubs in Michigan desperately wanted hope that their industries could finally get the revival they had not seen under previous administrations. Trump offered the hope they craved, promising a crowd of Michigan voters to "restore manufacturing in the United States." Plenty of presidential candidates have made claims like that, but Michiganders trusted Trump because they knew he would follow through on his promise.

The people of Michigan can see in hindsight how President Trump has followed through on his pledge. The numbers back him up. Under the Trump administration, workers in manufacturing enjoyed record-smashing growth. 2018 saw more manufacturing jobs added to the American economy than any previous year since Reagan. Manufacturing also rose as a percentage of total population for the first time since Reagan was in office. Trump does not need any excuses about robots taking over the manufacturing industry to explain away poor performance from the White House. The numbers speak for themselves. President Trump is proof that pro-business policy is all our workers need to thrive. By cutting taxes and securing good trade deals, the economic engine of American manufacturing might can roar to life. President Trump is doing what needs to be done to make this a reality for the people of Michigan and elsewhere.

Find out more about this Promise Kept by visiting PMPK2020.com

Promise #86
Run America Like His Own Business

Donald Trump was a true anomaly among presidential candidates. Americans were intrigued by the fact that he had never held public office before in his life. As a successful businessman, he certainly had a keen understanding of how politicians think, but he personally had always worked on his own business endeavors. When skeptics expressed nervousness about trusting their votes to someone who had no real track record in politics to point to, Trump countered by saying that his track record was how he had run his businesses. He promised to run our nation with the same tenacity, passion, and prudence as he had run his own businesses. President Trump's supporters and critics both agree that he has not acted like a traditional politician. From his mannerisms to his management style, Trump has not conformed to the mold left by previous ineffective administrations. When you boil it all down, Trump is not about business-as-usual. He's just the business of getting things done for the American people.

President Trump makes the tough calls any businessman has to make. He has trimmed bloating budgets and passed those savings on to the American people. He has directed all departments of the federal government to pursue efficiency, effectiveness, and cost savings. When was the last time you saw a sentence with the words "federal government" and "cost savings" in the same sentence? Only a businessman like President Trump could make that a reality.

Find out more about this Promise Kept by visiting PMPK2020.com

Promise #87
Save Families From Having Loved Ones Killed By Illegal Aliens

Under their stated goal, ICE's Enforcement and Removal Operations (ERO) activity "identifies, arrests, and removes aliens who present a danger to national security or a threat to public safety, or who otherwise undermine border control and the integrity of the U.S. immigration system." This important mission is accented by the tragic stream of stories detailing the crimes of illegal aliens against American citizens. America was rocked by the tragic death of Kate Steinle at the hands of an illegal alien, but she is only the public face of a much larger problem. Recent numbers from the Bureau of Justice Statistics show that two-thirds of all federal arrests are for non-U.S. citizens. Those are not just immigration crimes, either. Non-citizens account for a full one-quarter of drug arrests, property arrests, and fraud arrests. In 2018, 500 non-citizens were convicted of murder on American shores. President Obama may have ignored these tragedies, but Donald Trump promised to stop the killing.

President Trump jumped into action as soon as he took office. He began massively increasing the number of ICE agents in 2017. By the end of 2018, he had increased the number of ICE arrests by nearly 50% when compared to 2016 numbers. The Trump administration has made it a priority to protect American families from the danger of illegal alien criminals. He knows how to put "America First" to work.

Promise #88
Scale Back Department of Education

Many politicians see the Department of Education as untouchable. After all, who wants to be the candidate against education? Donald Trump was not only bold enough to stand up to the Department of Education as a candidate, but he was also wise enough to draw a clear line between the federal Department of Education and locally controlled education. The constant theme of the Trump campaign was to return power back to the states and local school boards by scaling back the Department of Education. True to his word, President Trump instructed his Department of Education under Betsy DeVos to make major cuts. He instituted a hiring freeze and proposed budgets with reduced funding. As an added means of increasing efficiency, he proposed rolling together several programs within the department.

The biggest myth in education is that throwing more money at the problem will always fix it. This kind of rudimentary thinking is completely counterintuitive, yet teachers unions spread the myth to line their own pockets. The real solution to the problem is getting the federal government out of it. Parents know what is best for their own children. Returning power over education to the local level is the best way to ensure efficiency and effectiveness within the public schools. That is the path Donald Trump campaigned on, and it is the policy President Trump has consistently stood by throughout his administration.

Find out more about this Promise Kept by visiting PMPK2020.com

Promise #89
Scale Back EPA

When asked how he would fund his tax cuts, President Trump listed off a litany of departments he would significantly cut. Among those was the Environmental Protection Agency (EPA). Speaking to that end, Trump said, "We are going to get rid of it in almost every form. We're going to have little tidbits left, but we're going to take a tremendous amount out." Trump's plan draws a stark contrast between the activities of the EPA and necessary conservation efforts. The EPA is infamous for harassing businesses, slowing progress on needed industrial projects, and bullying property owners. Nothing brings more dread to the heart of a construction crew than a call from the EPA. Some of their functions can be useful, but like any other bloated government bureaucracy, they seek only to expand their power and regulate businesses out of existence. They feel they have to justify their own existence in order to pull in more funding. Meanwhile, American businesses often have no recourse when bullied by the EPA. They could try to spar with the EPA in court, but an army of government lawyers with bottomless coffers would be waiting to send them packing.

President Trump put a stop to this egregious bullying. As of July 2020, Trump had reversed a total of sixty-eight burdensome environmental rules. With thirty-two other repeals in process, that is a total of one hundred terrible rules blotted out of the books.

Find out more about this Promise Kept by visiting PMPK2020.com

Promise #90
Simplify The Tax Code

Americans should not have to turn Tax Day into Tax Month for all of the complicated paperwork it requires. Candidate Donald Trump's tax plan promised to, "Simplify the tax code to reduce the headaches Americans face in preparing their taxes." That certainly sounds like a tall order. Skeptics shrugged it off as an empty campaign promise. However, the Tax Cuts and Jobs Act of 2017 tangibly simplified the tax preparation process for millions of Americans in every income bracket. The key to simplifying the tax code rested in the nearly doubled standard deduction. When filing for taxes, individuals have the option to reduce their taxable income by an array of little deductions including one for charitable giving and one for interest on a mortgage. This is called an "itemized deduction." Conversely, you can give up the itemized deduction by taking a "standard deduction," which is the same for everyone regardless of personal circumstances.

President Trump increased the standard deduction from $6,500 to $13,000 per person. Consequently, 28.5 million filers saved more money taking the standard deduction instead of the itemized deduction. And they saved the hassle involved with itemizing a bunch of small deductions. The IRS reported this change would save Americans an average of 4-7% of the hassle involved with filing taxes. That might not seem like a lot, but it adds up to between $3.1 and $5.4 billion in compliance savings for American taxpayers.

Find out more about this Promise Kept by visiting PMPK2020.com

Promise #91
Start Winning Again

In 2016, Americans were tired of feeling like losers. Endless wars in the Middle East, being swindled by China on trade, and suffering through stunted economic growth all caused people to begin thinking America's best days were behind her. We had been told that our manufacturing jobs were never coming back, that American exceptionalism was a lie, and that our history was something to be ashamed of. Donald Trump spread a different message. He proclaimed that America could be great again. He unapologetically defended our nation with his bold America First policy. Much like when President Reagan's policy with regards to the Soviet Union was "We win, they lose," Trump declared that America would start winning again.

As president, Donald Trump declared to the world that things are changing under his administration. He got tough in trade negotiations, delivering one solid deal after another. He set about to rebuild our nation's Armed Forces as the greatest fighting force in the world. He revived our nation's manufacturing sector. The nation's economy is roaring to life as never before in spite of current challenges. Nations who had long considered America to be washed up are changing their tune. As President Trump said to graduates at the U.S. Naval Academy, "Our country has regained the respect that we used to have long ago. Yes, they are respecting us again. America is back."

Promise #92
Strengthen Our Military

Candidate Donald Trump fully embraced military superiority in the months leading up to his election. On the campaign trail, he pointed out how American military might has declined substantially since the end of the Cold War, even though the foreign threats are more deadly than ever before. He pledged to rebuild the American military to adequately face global threats in the world today with overwhelming force. President Trump got the chance to deliver with the National Defense Authorization Act of 2019. In it, Trump authorized an expansion of military personnel by 15,600 troops. Additionally, he gave the troops a bigger pay raise than they had seen in nearly a decade. On top of that, he streamlined the Armed Forces to maintain our fighting capabilities at minimal cost. However, the hallmark of the legislation was its robust provisions dealing with space defense. In it, the U.S. Space Command was officially established under the U.S. Strategic Command. The American dream of protecting our interests beyond Earth's atmosphere was finally within our grasp.

A dealmaker like President Trump can appreciate the need to make our bargaining position as advantageous as possible. By building up our nation's military, Trump not only protects American lives, but also creates a deterrent to force potential aggressors to the bargaining table so our nation's heroes never have to be put in danger in the first place.

Find out more about this Promise Kept by visiting PMPK2020.com

Promise #93
Support Nuclear Power Generation

Candidate Donald Trump has been a full-throated supporter of nuclear power generation for years. Even back in 2011, he called himself "very strongly in favor of nuclear energy." He promised that he would give his full support to development of nuclear energy technology as president, in addition to supporting traditional fuel sources like natural gas and coal. As he pointed out, there is a time and a place for all kinds of energy technologies. We just have to be smart about which we use where and allow American innovation to lead the way with new solutions. In the spirit of that position, President Trump signed the Nuclear Energy Innovation Capabilities Act in October 2018 to give nuclear technology the room to grow. It calls for public-private partnership in the form of cost-sharing grants to cover licensing fees. It also calls for the Department of Energy to expand research into nuclear power and to expand reactor fuel testing capabilities.

All that may sound highly technical, but it all boils down to this: nuclear power generation is the best way to consistently generate power with zero carbon emissions. Modern technology has revolutionized the safety standards for these reactors, making a meltdown nearly impossible. If America does not start expanding our nuclear capabilities, we will fall hopelessly behind other nations who are making the smart choices. Under President Trump, America is back on the right track.

Find out more about this Promise Kept by visiting PMPK2020.com

Promise #94
Suspend Immigration From Terrorism-Prone Nations

The primary purpose of any government should be the protection of its citizens. For far too long, our nation placed the preferences of prospective immigrants ahead of our own interests and would allow people to come from very dangerous parts of the world with very minimal vetting. Donald Trump promised to halt immigration from these terrorist hotspots until our nation could find a better way to employ "extreme vetting" for anyone coming to our shores. President Trump quickly followed through on his promise by issuing an executive order all but banning travel from terrorist hotspots like Iran, Iraq, Libya, Somalia, Sudan, Syria, and Yemen. Immediately, leftists went to court in the hopes that judges would overturn the will of the people when they elected Donald Trump. Trump then issued a new order removing Iraq and Sudan from the list, while adding Chad, North Korea, and Venezuela. So far, the courts have yet to overrule this updated order. President Trump then expanded the travel ban to reinstate the ban on Sudan while including other terrorism-prone nations like Eritrea, Kyrgyzstan, Myanmar, Nigeria, and Tanzania.

If we are going to put Americans first, bold action must be taken on immigration policy. When it comes to nationals from countries harboring known terrorists, the policy of the U.S. government should be to employ extreme vetting. President Trump is right to stop immigration from these nations until proper vetting becomes a reality.

Find out more about this Promise Kept by visiting PMPK2020.com

Promise #95
Take Care Of Women

Despite what certain highly compensated celebrities might say, feminism does not speak for all women. Feminism only speaks for feminists. Donald Trump did not identify as a feminist, but he promised, "I will take care of women, and I have great respect for women." Of course, saying that only infuriated feminists all the more, but Trump stood by his pledge. As president, Donald Trump has been a champion for real rights for women. His tax cuts benefited women by providing new jobs and simplifying the tax code. American families also saw a massive increase in the child care tax credit, which gives parents the power to decide how to use their money to raise their children. As a defender of the Second Amendment, President Trump makes it easier for women, who have a natural physical disadvantage to men, to defend themselves with the great equalizer. He empowers them by allowing them to empower themselves, unlike previous anti-gun administrations. Trump also protects women by making law and order a priority.

While President Trump gives women actual progress, feminists still whine about how women need liberal agenda items like the phony Equal Rights Amendment. Women throughout our nation are waking up to the fact that the feminist movement does not speak for them. If they want real progress and real equality, the conservative policies of President Trump are their very best ally.

Find out more about this Promise Kept by visiting PMPK2020.com

Promise #96
Take No Salary

Donald Trump makes no bones about his personal wealth. With a net worth of $2.1 billion, he is officially our nation's first billionaire president. The left tries endlessly to turn middle and lower class Americans against the wealthy, hoping that they can weaponize envy as a way to pick up more votes. Trump countered this move by saying his wealth was not only an indicator of his abilities as a businessman, but a sign of his independence. As an independently wealthy person, he contended that he did not have to rely on wealthy people to fund his campaigns or his lifestyle. To cement his altruistic intentions in seeking the Oval Office, he promised "The first thing I'm gonna do is tell you that if I'm elected president, I'm accepting no salary. Okay? That's not a big deal for me."

Technically speaking, federal law requires the president to be compensated. However, President Trump gets around that by donating one-fourth of his annual salary to some department of the federal government every quarter. So far, he's given to the National Parks Service, the VA, HHS, and more. Recently, he's been donating his salary to help fight COVID-19. If giving money back to the federal government isn't a sign of Trump's desire to be a true public servant, I don't know what is. Anyone who is willing to lose money in order to work as hard as President Trump is worthy of our respect.

Promise #97
Establish Space Force

When President Ronald Reagan called for the United States to build defensive weapons in space, he was ridiculed mercilessly. Opponents labelled his Strategic Defense Initiative "Star Wars," hoping that their mockery would drown out the scientists and military leaders who knew Reagan's plan was both possible and desperately needed. Although Reagan's dream never came true, the threat of space warfare has not gone away. America has a tremendous amount of interests in space, including key communication, GPS, and weather satellites, yet we have absolutely zero defenses for these interests aside from retaliation here on Earth. Nations like China and Russia are working right now to develop anti-satellite weapons. President Donald Trump recognized this threat. Once again, anti-defense politicians and pundits countered the bold vision of space defense with mockery and derision. This time, their underhanded tactics did not work. The 2020 National Defense Authorization Act gave President Trump the funds he needed to officially establish the sixth branch of the U.S. Armed Forces, known as the U.S. Space Force.

President Trump is a man who demands to be taken seriously. When it comes to defending the American people, he is willing to take bold action to fight any threat, foreign or domestic. Future generations will thank President Trump for his strategic, far-thinking vision for the protection of American interests beyond Earth's atmosphere.

Find out more about this Promise Kept by visiting PMPK2020.com

Promise #98
Use Tariffs On China

Donald Trump made it clear that China will either start following the rules, or they would face stiff tariffs. Their unfair trade practices, he warned, are clear violations of the agreement that enabled China to enter the World Trade Organization in 2001. Trump did not want China to think he would be another American politician eager to roll over for the communist regime. He dramatically said, "We're not playing games any longer, folks." While other presidents might have feared confronting China on their gross economic abuses, President Trump tackled them head-on. After officially designating them a currency manipulator, the Trump administration imposed widespread tariffs on Chinese goods. In response, China imposed tariffs of their own. Rather than following the pattern of previous presidents by capitulating at the first sign of Chinese aggression, Trump doubled down with another round of tariffs. Although the tense situation brought on the ire of many Trump critics, he maintained that China had to be forced to stop taking advantage of the American people.

Just as President Trump predicted, China came to the bargaining table. President Trump's team worked to sign a "phase one" trade deal to see tariffs lifted. COVID-19 interrupted any further progress on China trade deals, but President Trump has officially proven that tariffs can be a successful tool to secure authentically free trade for the American people.

Find out more about this Promise Kept by visiting PMPK2020.com

Promise #99
Withdraw From Paris Climate Accords

Donald Trump has a way of carefully crafting a point to resonate with the American people. When he promised to leave the Paris Climate Agreement, he said it was because "My job is to represent the people of Pittsburgh, not the people of Paris." Quickly, withdrawing from the Agreement became an integral part of his America First message. The American people called for the withdrawal for a number of reasons. First, the Paris Agreement is totally ineffective. Research indicates that even if every nation followed every stipulation of the document to the letter—an unlikely prospect—global temperatures would only be cooled by 0.36 degrees Fahrenheit by the year 2100. Furthermore, the Agreement would burden American manufacturers with undue expenses and restrictions. Since many other nations openly violate these sorts of agreements, the U.S. would be left behind.

Perhaps most egregiously, the Paris Climate Agreement was hated because it was not an "agreement" at all. By every conventional definition, it was a treaty. However, President Obama refused to call it a treaty because that would have subjected it to approval by the Senate. So, in a semantic bid to flout the Constitution, he claimed the treaty was really just an "accord," even though it would dramatically affect U.S. policy and every American. Thankfully, President Trump heard the outcry of the American people and formally withdrew the U.S. from the Paris Climate Agreement on November 4, 2019.

Find out more about this Promise Kept by visiting PMPK2020.com

Promise #100
Make America Great Again

Four simple words defined the 2016 Trump presidential campaign: Make America Great Again. It's a simple phrase, but one with a lot of meaning behind it. After eight years under President Obama, Americans were tired of being told their nation was not great. We all remember the infamous April 2009 interview in which Obama condescendingly said, "I believe in American exceptionalism, just as I suspect that the Brits believe in British exceptionalism and the Greeks believe in Greek exceptionalism." That kind of dismissive attitude toward American greatness is what patriots throughout our nation were tired of. President Trump cast a different vision for the people of America. He promised to restore the American greatness politicians on both sides of the aisle spent decades trying to bury. However, President Trump has done much more than make promises. He consistently works to keep the promises he made on the campaign trail. People may say Trump is unpredictable, but they are wrong. If you want to know what Trump will do, just look at what he said he would do. It's just that easy.

The singular aim of the Trump administration has been to restore the greatness enjoyed by our nation in the days our parents and grandparents told us about. We have so much more to look forward to. Donald Trump believes the best days of America are still ahead. He has proven that to be so with every promise he has kept.

Find out more about this Promise Kept by visiting PMPK2020.com

Epic
Trump Speeches

Remarks at 72nd Session of the United Nations General Assembly
September 19, 2017
New York City

Mr. Secretary General, Mr. President, world leaders, and distinguished delegates: Welcome to New York. It is a profound honor to stand here in my home city, as a representative of the American people, to address the people of the world.

As millions of our citizens continue to suffer the effects of the devastating hurricanes that have struck our country, I want to begin by expressing my appreciation to every leader in this room who has offered assistance and aid. The American people are strong and resilient, and they will emerge from these hardships more determined than ever before.

Fortunately, the United States has done very well since Election Day last November 8th. The stock market is at an all-time high—a record. Unemployment is at its lowest level in 16 years, and because of our regulatory and other reforms, we have more people working in the United States today than ever before. Companies are moving back, creating job growth the likes of which our country has not seen in a very long time. And it has just been announced that we will be spending almost $700 billion on our military and defense.

Our military will soon be the strongest it has ever been. For more than 70 years, in times of war and peace, the leaders of nations, movements, and religions have stood before this assembly. Like them, I intend to address some of the very serious threats before us today but also the enormous potential waiting to be unleashed.

We live in a time of extraordinary opportunity. Breakthroughs in science, technology, and medicine are curing illnesses and solving problems that prior generations thought impossible to solve.

But each day also brings news of growing dangers that threaten everything we cherish and value. Terrorists and extremists have gathered strength and spread to every region of the planet. Rogue regimes represented in this body not only support terrorists but threaten other nations and their own people with the most destructive weapons known to humanity.

Authority and authoritarian powers seek to collapse the values, the systems, and alliances that prevented conflict and tilted the world toward freedom since World War II.

International criminal networks traffic drugs, weapons, people; force dislocation and mass migration; threaten our borders; and new forms of aggression exploit technology to menace our citizens.

To put it simply, we meet at a time of both of immense promise and great peril. It is entirely up to us whether we lift the world to new heights, or let it fall into a valley of disrepair.

We have it in our power, should we so choose, to lift millions from poverty, to help our citizens realize their dreams, and to ensure that new generations of children are raised free from violence, hatred, and fear.

This institution was founded in the aftermath of two world wars to help shape this better future. It was based on the vision that diverse nations could cooperate to protect their sovereignty, preserve their security, and promote their prosperity.

It was in the same period, exactly 70 years ago, that the United States developed the Marshall Plan to help restore Europe. Those three beautiful pillars—they're pillars of peace, sovereignty, security, and prosperity.

The Marshall Plan was built on the noble idea that the whole world is safer when nations are strong, independent, and free. As President Truman said in his message to Congress at that time, "Our support of European recovery is in full accord with our support of the United Nations. The success of the United Nations depends upon the independent strength of its members."

To overcome the perils of the present and to achieve the promise of the future, we must begin with the wisdom of the past. Our success depends on a coalition of strong and independent nations that embrace their sovereignty to promote security, prosperity, and peace for themselves and for the world.

We do not expect diverse countries to share the same cultures, traditions, or even systems of government. But we do expect all nations to uphold these two core sovereign duties: to respect the interests of their own people and the rights of every other sovereign nation. This is the beautiful vision of this institution, and this is foundation for cooperation and success.

Strong, sovereign nations let diverse countries with different values, different cultures, and different dreams not just coexist, but work side by side on the basis of mutual respect.

Strong, sovereign nations let their people take ownership of the future and control their own destiny. And strong, sovereign nations allow individuals to flourish in the fullness of the life intended by God.

In America, we do not seek to impose our way of life on anyone, but rather to let it shine as an example for everyone to watch. This week gives our country a special reason to take pride in that example. We are celebrating the 230th anniversary of our beloved Constitution—the oldest constitution still in use in the world today.

This timeless document has been the foundation of peace, prosperity, and freedom for the Americans and for countless millions around the globe whose own countries have found inspiration in its respect for human nature, human dignity, and the rule of law.

The greatest in the United States Constitution is its first three beautiful words. They are: "We the people."

Generations of Americans have sacrificed to maintain the promise of those words, the promise of our country, and of our great history. In America, the people govern, the people rule, and the people are sovereign. I was elected not to take power, but to give power to the American people, where it belongs.

In foreign affairs, we are renewing this founding principle of sovereignty. Our government's first duty is to its people, to our citizens—to serve their needs, to ensure their safety, to preserve their rights, and to defend their values.

As President of the United States, I will always put America first, just like you, as the leaders of your countries will always, and should always, put your countries first. (Applause.)

All responsible leaders have an obligation to serve their own citizens, and the nation-state remains the best vehicle for elevating the human condition.

But making a better life for our people also requires us to work together in close harmony and unity to create a more safe and peaceful future for all people.

The United States will forever be a great friend to the world, and especially to its allies. But we can no longer be taken advantage of, or enter into a one-sided deal where the United States gets nothing in return. As long as I hold this office, I will defend America's interests above all else.

But in fulfilling our obligations to our own nations, we also realize that it's in everyone's interest to seek a future where all nations can be sovereign, prosperous, and secure.

America does more than speak for the values expressed in the United Nations Charter. Our citizens have paid the ultimate price to defend our freedom and the freedom of many nations represented in this great hall. America's devotion is measured on the battlefields where our young men and women have fought and sacrificed alongside of our allies, from the beaches of Europe to the deserts of the Middle East to the jungles of Asia.

It is an eternal credit to the American character that even after we and our allies emerged victorious from the bloodiest war in history, we did not seek territorial expansion, or attempt to oppose and impose our way of life on others. Instead, we helped build institutions such as this one to defend the sovereignty, security, and prosperity for all.

For the diverse nations of the world, this is our hope. We want harmony and friendship, not conflict and strife. We are guided by outcomes, not ideology. We have a policy of principled realism, rooted in shared goals, interests, and values.

That realism forces us to confront a question facing every leader and nation in this room. It is a question we cannot escape or avoid. We will slide down the path of complacency, numb to the challenges, threats, and even wars that we face. Or do we have enough strength and pride to confront those dangers today, so that our citizens can enjoy peace and prosperity tomorrow?

If we desire to lift up our citizens, if we aspire to the approval of history, then we must fulfill our sovereign duties to the people we faithfully represent. We must protect our nations, their interests, and their futures. We must reject threats to sovereignty, from the Ukraine to the South China Sea. We must uphold respect for law, respect for borders, and respect for culture, and the peaceful engagement these allow. And just as the founders of this body intended, we must work together and confront together those who threaten us with chaos, turmoil, and terror.

The scourge of our planet today is a small group of rogue regimes that violate every principle on which the United Nations is based. They respect neither their own citizens nor the sovereign rights of their countries.

If the righteous many do not confront the wicked few, then evil will triumph. When decent people and nations become bystanders to history, the forces of destruction only gather power and strength.

No one has shown more contempt for other nations and for the wellbeing of their own people than the depraved regime in North Korea. It is responsible for the starvation deaths of millions of North Koreans, and for the imprisonment, torture, killing, and oppression of countless more.

We were all witness to the regime's deadly abuse when an innocent American college student, Otto Warmbier, was returned to America only to die a few days later. We saw it in the assassination of the dictator's brother using banned nerve agents in an international airport. We know it kidnapped a sweet 13-year-old Japanese girl from a beach in her own country to enslave her as a language tutor for North Korea's spies.

If this is not twisted enough, now North Korea's reckless pursuit of nuclear weapons and ballistic missiles threatens the entire world with unthinkable loss of human life.

It is an outrage that some nations would not only trade with such a regime, but would arm, supply, and financially support a country that imperils the world with nuclear conflict. No nation on earth has an interest in seeing this band of criminals arm itself with nuclear weapons and missiles.

The United States has great strength and patience, but if it is forced to defend itself or its allies, we will have no choice but to totally destroy North Korea. Rocket Man is on a suicide mission for himself and for his regime. The United States is ready, willing and able, but hopefully this will not be necessary. That's what the United Nations is all about; that's what the United Nations is for. Let's see how they do.

It is time for North Korea to realize that the denuclearization is its only acceptable future. The United Nations Security Council recently held two unanimous 15-0 votes adopting hard-hitting resolutions against North Korea, and I want to thank China and Russia for joining the vote to impose sanctions, along with all of the other members of the Security Council. Thank you to all involved.

But we must do much more. It is time for all nations to work together to isolate the Kim regime until it ceases its hostile behavior.

We face this decision not only in North Korea. It is far past time for the nations of the world to confront another reckless regime—one that speaks openly of mass murder, vowing death to America, destruction to Israel, and ruin for many leaders and nations in this room.

The Iranian government masks a corrupt dictatorship behind the false guise of a democracy. It has turned a wealthy country with a rich history and culture into an economically depleted rogue state whose chief exports are violence, bloodshed, and chaos. The longest-suffering victims of Iran's leaders are, in fact, its own people.

Rather than use its resources to improve Iranian lives, its oil profits go to fund Hezbollah and other terrorists that kill innocent Muslims and attack their peaceful Arab and Israeli neighbors. This wealth, which rightly belongs to Iran's people, also goes to shore up Bashar al-Assad's dictatorship, fuel Yemen's civil war, and undermine peace throughout the entire Middle East.

We cannot let a murderous regime continue these destabilizing activities while building dangerous missiles, and we cannot abide by an agreement if it provides cover for the eventual construction of a nuclear program. (Applause.) The Iran Deal was one of the worst and most one-sided transactions the United States has ever entered into. Frankly, that deal is an embarrassment to the United States, and I don't think you've heard the last of it—believe me.

It is time for the entire world to join us in demanding that Iran's government end its pursuit of death and destruction. It is time for the regime to free all Americans and citizens of other nations that they have unjustly detained. And above all, Iran's government must stop supporting terrorists, begin serving its own people, and respect the sovereign rights of its neighbors.

The entire world understands that the good people of Iran want change, and, other than the vast military power of the United States, that Iran's people are what their leaders fear the most. This is what causes the regime to restrict Internet access, tear down satellite dishes, shoot unarmed student protestors, and imprison political reformers.

Oppressive regimes cannot endure forever, and the day will come when the Iranian people will face a choice. Will they continue down the path of poverty, bloodshed, and terror? Or will the Iranian people return to the nation's proud roots as a center of civilization, culture, and wealth where their people can be happy and prosperous once again?

107

The Iranian regime's support for terror is in stark contrast to the recent commitments of many of its neighbors to fight terrorism and halt its financing.

In Saudi Arabia early last year, I was greatly honored to address the leaders of more than 50 Arab and Muslim nations. We agreed that all responsible nations must work together to confront terrorists and the Islamist extremism that inspires them.

We will stop radical Islamic terrorism because we cannot allow it to tear up our nation, and indeed to tear up the entire world.

We must deny the terrorists safe haven, transit, funding, and any form of support for their vile and sinister ideology. We must drive them out of our nations. It is time to expose and hold responsible those countries who support and finance terror groups like al Qaeda, Hezbollah, the Taliban and others that slaughter innocent people.

The United States and our allies are working together throughout the Middle East to crush the loser terrorists and stop the reemergence of safe havens they use to launch attacks on all of our people.

Last month, I announced a new strategy for victory in the fight against this evil in Afghanistan. From now on, our security interests will dictate the length and scope of military operations, not arbitrary benchmarks and timetables set up by politicians.

I have also totally changed the rules of engagement in our fight against the Taliban and other terrorist groups. In Syria and Iraq, we have made big gains toward lasting defeat of ISIS. In fact, our country has achieved more against ISIS in the last eight months than it has in many, many years combined.

We seek the de-escalation of the Syrian conflict, and a political solution that honors the will of the Syrian people. The actions of the criminal regime of Bashar al-Assad, including the use of chemical weapons against his own citizens—even innocent children—shock the conscience of every decent person. No society can be safe if banned chemical weapons are allowed to spread. That is why the United States carried out a missile strike on the airbase that launched the attack.

We appreciate the efforts of United Nations agencies that are providing vital humanitarian assistance in areas liberated from ISIS, and we especially thank Jordan, Turkey and Lebanon for their role in hosting refugees from the Syrian conflict.

The United States is a compassionate nation and has spent billions and billions of dollars in helping to support this effort. We seek an approach to refugee resettlement that is designed to help these horribly treated people, and which enables their eventual return to their home countries, to be part of the rebuilding process.

For the cost of resettling one refugee in the United States, we can assist more than 10 in their home region. Out of the goodness of our hearts, we offer financial assistance to hosting countries in the region, and we support recent agreements of the G20 nations that will seek to host refugees as close to their home countries as possible. This is the safe, responsible, and humanitarian approach.

For decades, the United States has dealt with migration challenges here in the Western Hemisphere. We have learned that, over the long term, uncontrolled migration is deeply unfair to both the sending and the receiving countries.

For the sending countries, it reduces domestic pressure to pursue needed political and economic reform, and drains them of the human capital necessary to motivate and implement those reforms.

For the receiving countries, the substantial costs of uncontrolled migration are borne overwhelmingly by low-income citizens whose concerns are often ignored by both media and government.

I want to salute the work of the United Nations in seeking to address the problems that cause people to flee from their homes. The United Nations and African Union led peacekeeping missions to have invaluable contributions in stabilizing conflicts in Africa. The United States continues to lead the world in humanitarian assistance, including famine prevention and relief in South Sudan, Somalia, and northern Nigeria and Yemen.

We have invested in better health and opportunity all over the world through programs like PEPFAR, which funds AIDS relief; the President's Malaria Initiative; the Global Health Security Agenda; the Global Fund to End Modern Slavery; and the Women Entrepreneurs Finance Initiative, part of our commitment to empowering women all across the globe.

We also thank—(applause)—we also thank the Secretary General for recognizing that the United Nations must reform if it is to be an effective partner in confronting threats to sovereignty, security, and prosperity. Too often the focus of this organization has not been on results, but on bureaucracy and process.

In some cases, states that seek to subvert this institution's noble aims have hijacked the very systems that are supposed to advance them. For example, it is a massive source of embarrassment to the United Nations that some governments with egregious human rights records sit on the U.N. Human Rights Council.

The United States is one out of 193 countries in the United Nations, and yet we pay 22 percent of the entire budget and more. In fact, we pay far more than anybody realizes. The United States bears an unfair cost burden, but, to be fair, if it could actually accomplish all of its stated goals, especially the goal of peace, this investment would easily be well worth it.

Major portions of the world are in conflict and some, in fact, are going to hell. But the powerful people in this room, under the guidance and auspices of the United Nations, can solve many of these vicious and complex problems.

The American people hope that one day soon the United Nations can be a much more accountable and effective advocate for human dignity and freedom around the world. In the meantime, we believe that no nation should have to bear a disproportionate share of the burden, militarily or financially. Nations of the world must take a greater role in promoting secure and prosperous societies in their own regions.

That is why in the Western Hemisphere, the United States has stood against the corrupt and destabilizing regime in Cuba and embraced the enduring dream of the Cuban people to live in freedom. My administration recently announced that we will not lift sanctions on the Cuban government until it makes fundamental reforms.

We have also imposed tough, calibrated sanctions on the socialist Maduro regime in Venezuela, which has brought a once thriving nation to the brink of total collapse.

The socialist dictatorship of Nicolas Maduro has inflicted terrible pain and suffering on the good people of that country. This corrupt regime destroyed a prosperous nation by imposing a failed ideology that has produced poverty and misery everywhere it has been tried. To make matters worse, Maduro has defied his own people, stealing power from their elected representatives to preserve his disastrous rule.

The Venezuelan people are starving and their country is collapsing. Their democratic institutions are being destroyed. This situation is completely unacceptable and we cannot stand by and watch.

As a responsible neighbor and friend, we and all others have a goal. That goal is to help them regain their freedom, recover their country, and restore their democracy. I would like to thank leaders in this room for condemning the regime and providing vital support to the Venezuelan people.

The United States has taken important steps to hold the regime accountable. We are prepared to take further action if the government of Venezuela persists on its path to impose authoritarian rule on the Venezuelan people.

We are fortunate to have incredibly strong and healthy trade relationships with many of the Latin American countries gathered here today. Our economic bond forms a critical foundation for advancing peace and prosperity for all of our people and all of our neighbors.

I ask every country represented here today to be prepared to do more to address this very real crisis. We call for the full restoration of democracy and political freedoms in Venezuela. (Applause.)

The problem in Venezuela is not that socialism has been poorly implemented, but that socialism has been faithfully implemented. (Applause.) From the Soviet Union to Cuba to Venezuela, wherever true socialism or communism has been adopted, it has delivered anguish and devastation and failure. Those who preach the tenets of these discredited ideologies only contribute to the continued suffering of the people who live under these cruel systems.

America stands with every person living under a brutal regime. Our respect for sovereignty is also a call for action. All people deserve a government that cares for their safety, their interests, and their wellbeing, including their prosperity.

In America, we seek stronger ties of business and trade with all nations of good will, but this trade must be fair and it must be reciprocal.

For too long, the American people were told that mammoth multinational trade deals, unaccountable international tribunals, and powerful global bureaucracies were the best way to promote their success. But as those promises flowed, millions of jobs vanished and thousands of factories disappeared. Others gamed the system and broke the rules. And our great middle class, once the bedrock of American prosperity, was forgotten and left behind, but they are forgotten no more and they will never be forgotten again.

While America will pursue cooperation and commerce with other nations, we are renewing our commitment to the first duty of every government: the duty of our citizens. This bond is the source of America's strength and that of every responsible nation represented here today.

If this organization is to have any hope of successfully confronting the challenges before us, it will depend, as President Truman said some 70 years ago, on the "independent strength of its members." If we are to embrace the opportunities of the future and overcome the present dangers together, there can be no substitute for strong, sovereign, and independent nations—nations that are rooted in their histories and invested in their destinies; nations that seek allies to befriend, not enemies to conquer; and most important of all, nations that are home to patriots, to men and women who are willing to sacrifice for their countries, their fellow citizens, and for all that is best in the human spirit.

In remembering the great victory that led to this body's founding, we must never forget that those heroes who fought against evil also fought for the nations that they loved.

Patriotism led the Poles to die to save Poland, the French to fight for a free France, and the Brits to stand strong for Britain.

Today, if we do not invest ourselves, our hearts, and our minds in our nations, if we will not build strong families, safe communities, and healthy societies for ourselves, no one can do it for us.

111

We cannot wait for someone else, for faraway countries or far-off bureaucrats—we can't do it. We must solve our problems, to build our prosperity, to secure our futures, or we will be vulnerable to decay, domination, and defeat.

The true question for the United Nations today, for people all over the world who hope for better lives for themselves and their children, is a basic one: Are we still patriots? Do we love our nations enough to protect their sovereignty and to take ownership of their futures? Do we revere them enough to defend their interests, preserve their cultures, and ensure a peaceful world for their citizens?

One of the greatest American patriots, John Adams, wrote that the American Revolution was "effected before the war commenced. The Revolution was in the minds and hearts of the people."

That was the moment when America awoke, when we looked around and understood that we were a nation. We realized who we were, what we valued, and what we would give our lives to defend. From its very first moments, the American story is the story of what is possible when people take ownership of their future.

The United States of America has been among the greatest forces for good in the history of the world, and the greatest defenders of sovereignty, security, and prosperity for all.

Now we are calling for a great reawakening of nations, for the revival of their spirits, their pride, their people, and their patriotism.

History is asking us whether we are up to the task. Our answer will be a renewal of will, a rediscovery of resolve, and a rebirth of devotion. We need to defeat the enemies of humanity and unlock the potential of life itself.

Our hope is a world and—world of proud, independent nations that embrace their duties, seek friendship, respect others, and make common cause in the greatest shared interest of all: a future of dignity and peace for the people of this wonderful Earth.

This is the true vision of the United Nations, the ancient wish of every people, and the deepest yearning that lives inside every sacred soul.

So let this be our mission, and let this be our message to the world: We will fight together, sacrifice together, and stand together for peace, for freedom, for justice, for family, for humanity, and for the almighty God who made us all.

Thank you. God bless you. God bless the nations of the world. And God bless the United States of America. Thank you very much. (Applause.)

**Remarks by President Trump to the
73rd Session of the United Nations General Assembly**
September 25, 2018
United Nations Headquarters, New York

Madam President, Mr. Secretary-General, world leaders, ambassadors, and distinguished delegates:

One year ago, I stood before you for the first time in this grand hall. I addressed the threats facing our world, and I presented a vision to achieve a brighter future for all of humanity.

Today, I stand before the United Nations General Assembly to share the extraordinary progress we've made.

In less than two years, my administration has accomplished more than almost any administration in the history of our country.

America's — so true. (Laughter.) Didn't expect that reaction, but that's okay. (Laughter and applause.)

America's economy is booming like never before. Since my election, we've added $10 trillion in wealth. The stock market is at an all-time high in history, and jobless claims are at a 50-year low. African American, Hispanic American, and Asian American unemployment have all achieved their lowest levels ever recorded. We've added more than 4 million new jobs, including half a million manufacturing jobs.

We have passed the biggest tax cuts and reforms in American history. We've started the construction of a major border wall, and we have greatly strengthened border security.

We have secured record funding for our military — $700 billion this year, and $716 billion next year. Our military will soon be more powerful than it has ever been before.

In other words, the United States is stronger, safer, and a richer country than it was when I assumed office less than two years ago.

We are standing up for America and for the American people. And we are also standing up for the world.

This is great news for our citizens and for peace-loving people everywhere. We believe that when nations respect the rights of their neighbors, and defend the interests of their people, they can better work together to secure the blessings of safety, prosperity, and peace.

Each of us here today is the emissary of a distinct culture, a rich history, and a people bound together by ties of memory, tradition, and the values that make our homelands like nowhere else on Earth.

That is why America will always choose independence and cooperation over global governance, control, and domination.

I honor the right of every nation in this room to pursue its own customs, beliefs, and traditions. The United States will not tell you how to live or work or worship.

We only ask that you honor our sovereignty in return.

From Warsaw to Brussels, to Tokyo to Singapore, it has been my highest honor to represent the United States abroad. I have forged close relationships and friendships and strong partnerships with the leaders of many nations in this room, and our approach has already yielded incredible change.

With support from many countries here today, we have engaged with North Korea to replace the specter of conflict with a bold and new push for peace.

In June, I traveled to Singapore to meet face to face with North Korea's leader, Chairman Kim Jong Un.

We had highly productive conversations and meetings, and we agreed that it was in both countries' interest to pursue the denuclearization of the Korean Peninsula. Since that meeting, we have already seen a number of encouraging measures that few could have imagined only a short time ago.

The missiles and rockets are no longer flying in every direction. Nuclear testing has stopped. Some military facilities are already being dismantled. Our hostages have been released. And as promised, the remains of our fallen heroes are being returned home to lay at rest in American soil.

I would like to thank Chairman Kim for his courage and for the steps he has taken, though much work remains to be done. The sanctions will stay in place until denuclearization occurs.

I also want to thank the many member states who helped us reach this moment — a moment that is actually far greater than people would understand; far greater — but for also their support and the critical support that we will all need going forward.

A special thanks to President Moon of South Korea, Prime Minister Abe of Japan, and President Xi of China.

In the Middle East, our new approach is also yielding great strides and very historic change.

Following my trip to Saudi Arabia last year, the Gulf countries opened a new center to target terrorist financing. They are enforcing new sanctions, working with us to identify and track terrorist networks, and taking more responsibility for fighting terrorism and extremism in their own region.

The UAE, Saudi Arabia, and Qatar have pledged billions of dollars to aid the people of Syria and Yemen. And they are pursuing multiple avenues to ending Yemen's horrible, horrific civil war.

Ultimately, it is up to the nations of the region to decide what kind of future they want for themselves and their children.

For that reason, the United States is working with the Gulf Cooperation Council, Jordan, and Egypt to establish a regional strategic alliance so that

Middle Eastern nations can advance prosperity, stability, and security across their home region.

Thanks to the United States military and our partnership with many of your nations, I am pleased to report that the bloodthirsty killers known as ISIS have been driven out from the territory they once held in Iraq and Syria. We will continue to work with friends and allies to deny radical Islamic terrorists any funding, territory or support, or any means of infiltrating our borders.

The ongoing tragedy in Syria is heartbreaking. Our shared goals must be the de-escalation of military conflict, along with a political solution that honors the will of the Syrian people. In this vein, we urge the United Nations-led peace process be reinvigorated. But, rest assured, the United States will respond if chemical weapons are deployed by the Assad regime.

I commend the people of Jordan and other neighboring countries for hosting refugees from this very brutal civil war.

As we see in Jordan, the most compassionate policy is to place refugees as close to their homes as possible to ease their eventual return to be part of the rebuilding process. This approach also stretches finite resources to help far more people, increasing the impact of every dollar spent.

Every solution to the humanitarian crisis in Syria must also include a strategy to address the brutal regime that has fueled and financed it: the corrupt dictatorship in Iran.

Iran's leaders sow chaos, death, and destruction. They do not respect their neighbors or borders, or the sovereign rights of nations. Instead, Iran's leaders plunder the nation's resources to enrich themselves and to spread mayhem across the Middle East and far beyond.

The Iranian people are rightly outraged that their leaders have embezzled billions of dollars from Iran's treasury, seized valuable portions of the economy, and looted the people's religious endowments, all to line their own pockets and send their proxies to wage war. Not good.

Iran's neighbors have paid a heavy toll for the region's [regime's] agenda of aggression and expansion. That is why so many countries in the Middle East strongly supported my decision to withdraw the United States from the horrible 2015 Iran Nuclear Deal and re-impose nuclear sanctions.

The Iran deal was a windfall for Iran's leaders. In the years since the deal was reached, Iran's military budget grew nearly 40 percent. The dictatorship used the funds to build nuclear-capable missiles, increase internal repression, finance terrorism, and fund havoc and slaughter in Syria and Yemen.

The United States has launched a campaign of economic pressure to deny the regime the funds it needs to advance its bloody agenda. Last month, we began re-imposing hard-hitting nuclear sanctions that had been lifted under the Iran deal. Additional sanctions will resume November 5th, and more will follow. And we're working with countries that import Iranian crude oil to cut their purchases substantially.

We cannot allow the world's leading sponsor of terrorism to possess the planet's most dangerous weapons. We cannot allow a regime that chants "Death to America," and that threatens Israel with annihilation, to possess the means to deliver a nuclear warhead to any city on Earth. Just can't do it.

We ask all nations to isolate Iran's regime as long as its aggression continues. And we ask all nations to support Iran's people as they struggle to reclaim their religious and righteous destiny.

This year, we also took another significant step forward in the Middle East. In recognition of every sovereign state to determine its own capital, I moved the U.S. Embassy in Israel to Jerusalem.

The United States is committed to a future of peace and stability in the region, including peace between the Israelis and the Palestinians. That aim is advanced, not harmed, by acknowledging the obvious facts.

America's policy of principled realism means we will not be held hostage to old dogmas, discredited ideologies, and so-called experts who have been proven wrong over the years, time and time again. This is true not only in matters of peace, but in matters of prosperity.

We believe that trade must be fair and reciprocal. The United States will not be taken advantage of any longer.

For decades, the United States opened its economy — the largest, by far, on Earth — with few conditions. We allowed foreign goods from all over the world to flow freely across our borders.

Yet, other countries did not grant us fair and reciprocal access to their markets in return. Even worse, some countries abused their openness to dump their products, subsidize their goods, target our industries, and manipulate their currencies to gain unfair advantage over our country. As a result, our trade deficit ballooned to nearly $800 billion a year.

For this reason, we are systematically renegotiating broken and bad trade deals.

Last month, we announced a groundbreaking U.S.-Mexico trade agreement. And just yesterday, I stood with President Moon to announce the successful completion of the brand new U.S.-Korea trade deal. And this is just the beginning.

Many nations in this hall will agree that the world trading system is in dire need of change. For example, countries were admitted to the World Trade Organization that violate every single principle on which the organization is based. While the United States and many other nations play by the rules, these countries use government-run industrial planning and state-owned enterprises to rig the system in their favor. They engage in relentless product dumping, forced technology transfer, and the theft of intellectual property.

The United States lost over 3 million manufacturing jobs, nearly a quarter of all steel jobs, and 60,000 factories after China joined the WTO. And we have racked up $13 trillion in trade deficits over the last two decades.

But those days are over. We will no longer tolerate such abuse. We will not allow our workers to be victimized, our companies to be cheated, and our wealth to be plundered and transferred. America will never apologize for protecting its citizens.

The United States has just announced tariffs on another $200 billion in Chinese-made goods for a total, so far, of $250 billion. I have great respect and affection for my friend, President Xi, but I have made clear our trade imbalance is just not acceptable. China's market distortions and the way they deal cannot be tolerated.

As my administration has demonstrated, America will always act in our national interest.

I spoke before this body last year and warned that the U.N. Human Rights Council had become a grave embarrassment to this institution, shielding egregious human rights abusers while bashing America and its many friends.

Our Ambassador to the United Nations, Nikki Haley, laid out a clear agenda for reform, but despite reported and repeated warnings, no action at all was taken.

So the United States took the only responsible course: We withdrew from the Human Rights Council, and we will not return until real reform is enacted.

For similar reasons, the United States will provide no support in recognition to the International Criminal Court. As far as America is concerned, the ICC has no jurisdiction, no legitimacy, and no authority. The ICC claims near-universal jurisdiction over the citizens of every country, violating all principles of justice, fairness, and due process. We will never surrender America's sovereignty to an unelected, unaccountable, global bureaucracy.

America is governed by Americans. We reject the ideology of globalism, and we embrace the doctrine of patriotism.

Around the world, responsible nations must defend against threats to sovereignty not just from global governance, but also from other, new forms of coercion and domination.

In America, we believe strongly in energy security for ourselves and for our allies. We have become the largest energy producer anywhere on the face of the Earth.

The United States stands ready to export our abundant, affordable supply of oil, clean coal, and natural gas.

OPEC and OPEC nations, are, as usual, ripping off the rest of the world, and I don't like it. Nobody should like it. We defend many of these nations for nothing, and then they take advantage of us by giving us high oil prices. Not good.

We want them to stop raising prices, we want them to start lowering prices, and they must contribute substantially to military protection from now on. We are not going to put up with it — these horrible prices — much longer.

Reliance on a single foreign supplier can leave a nation vulnerable to extortion and intimidation. That is why we congratulate European states, such as Poland, for leading the construction of a Baltic pipeline so that nations are not dependent on Russia to meet their energy needs. Germany will become totally dependent on Russian energy if it does not immediately change course.

Here in the Western Hemisphere, we are committed to maintaining our independence from the encroachment of expansionist foreign powers.

It has been the formal policy of our country since President Monroe that we reject the interference of foreign nations in this hemisphere and in our own affairs. The United States has recently strengthened our laws to better screen foreign investments in our country for national security threats, and we welcome cooperation with countries in this region and around the world that wish to do the same. You need to do it for your own protection.

The United States is also working with partners in Latin America to confront threats to sovereignty from uncontrolled migration. Tolerance for human struggling and human smuggling and trafficking is not humane. It's a horrible thing that's going on, at levels that nobody has ever seen before. It's very, very cruel.

Illegal immigration funds criminal networks, ruthless gangs, and the flow of deadly drugs. Illegal immigration exploits vulnerable populations, hurts hardworking citizens, and has produced a vicious cycle of crime, violence, and poverty. Only by upholding national borders, destroying criminal gangs, can we break this cycle and establish a real foundation for prosperity.

We recognize the right of every nation in this room to set its own immigration policy in accordance with its national interests, just as we ask other countries to respect our own right to do the same — which we are doing. That is one reason the United States will not participate in the new Global Compact on Migration. Migration should not be governed by an international body unaccountable to our own citizens.

Ultimately, the only long-term solution to the migration crisis is to help people build more hopeful futures in their home countries. Make their countries great again.

Currently, we are witnessing a human tragedy, as an example, in Venezuela. More than 2 million people have fled the anguish inflicted by the socialist Maduro regime and its Cuban sponsors.

Not long ago, Venezuela was one of the richest countries on Earth. Today, socialism has bankrupted the oil-rich nation and driven its people into abject poverty.

Virtually everywhere socialism or communism has been tried, it has produced suffering, corruption, and decay. Socialism's thirst for power leads to expansion, incursion, and oppression. All nations of the world should resist socialism and the misery that it brings to everyone.

In that spirit, we ask the nations gathered here to join us in calling for the restoration of democracy in Venezuela. Today, we are announcing additional sanctions against the repressive regime, targeting Maduro's inner circle and close advisors.

We are grateful for all the work the United Nations does around the world to help people build better lives for themselves and their families.

The United States is the world's largest giver in the world, by far, of foreign aid. But few give anything to us. That is why we are taking a hard look at U.S. foreign assistance. That will be headed up by Secretary of State Mike Pompeo. We will examine what is working, what is not working, and whether the countries who receive our dollars and our protection also have our interests at heart.

Moving forward, we are only going to give foreign aid to those who respect us and, frankly, are our friends. And we expect other countries to pay their fair share for the cost of their defense.

The United States is committed to making the United Nations more effective and accountable. I have said many times that the United Nations has unlimited potential. As part of our reform effort, I have told our negotiators that the United States will not pay more than 25 percent of the U.N. peacekeeping budget. This will encourage other countries to step up, get involved, and also share in this very large burden.

And we are working to shift more of our funding from assessed contributions to voluntary so that we can target American resources to the programs with the best record of success.

Only when each of us does our part and contributes our share can we realize the U.N.'s highest aspirations. We must pursue peace without fear, hope without despair, and security without apology.

Looking around this hall where so much history has transpired, we think of the many before us who have come here to address the challenges of their nations and of their times. And our thoughts turn to the same question that ran through all their speeches and resolutions, through every word and every hope. It is the question of what kind of world will we leave for our children and what kind of nations they will inherit.

The dreams that fill this hall today are as diverse as the people who have stood at this podium, and as varied as the countries represented right here in this body are. It really is something. It really is great, great history.

There is India, a free society over a billion people, successfully lifting countless millions out of poverty and into the middle class.

There is Saudi Arabia, where King Salman and the Crown Prince are pursuing bold new reforms.

There is Israel, proudly celebrating its 70th anniversary as a thriving democracy in the Holy Land.

In Poland, a great people are standing up for their independence, their security, and their sovereignty.

Many countries are pursuing their own unique visions, building their own hopeful futures, and chasing their own wonderful dreams of destiny, of legacy, and of a home.

The whole world is richer, humanity is better, because of this beautiful constellation of nations, each very special, each very unique, and each shining brightly in its part of the world.

In each one, we see awesome promise of a people bound together by a shared past and working toward a common future.

As for Americans, we know what kind of future we want for ourselves. We know what kind of a nation America must always be.

In America, we believe in the majesty of freedom and the dignity of the individual. We believe in self-government and the rule of law. And we prize the culture that sustains our liberty — a culture built on strong families, deep faith, and fierce independence. We celebrate our heroes, we treasure our traditions, and above all, we love our country.

Inside everyone in this great chamber today, and everyone listening all around the globe, there is the heart of a patriot that feels the same powerful love for your nation, the same intense loyalty to your homeland.

The passion that burns in the hearts of patriots and the souls of nations has inspired reform and revolution, sacrifice and selflessness, scientific breakthroughs, and magnificent works of art.

Our task is not to erase it, but to embrace it. To build with it. To draw on its ancient wisdom. And to find within it the will to make our nations greater, our regions safer, and the world better.

To unleash this incredible potential in our people, we must defend the foundations that make it all possible. Sovereign and independent nations are the only vehicle where freedom has ever survived, democracy has ever endured, or peace has ever prospered. And so we must protect our sovereignty and our cherished independence above all.

When we do, we will find new avenues for cooperation unfolding before us. We will find new passion for peacemaking rising within us. We will find new purpose, new resolve, and new spirit flourishing all around us, and making this a more beautiful world in which to live.

So together, let us choose a future of patriotism, prosperity, and pride. Let us choose peace and freedom over domination and defeat. And let us come here to this place to stand for our people and their nations, forever strong, forever sovereign, forever just, and forever thankful for the grace and the goodness and the glory of God.

Thank you. God bless you. And God bless the nations of the world.

Thank you very much. Thank you. (Applause.

Remarks at 74th Session of the United Nations General Assembly
September 24, 2019
New York City

Thank you very much. Mr. President, Mr. Secretary-General, distinguished delegates, ambassadors, and world leaders:

Seven decades of history have passed through this hall, in all of their richness and drama. Where I stand, the world has heard from presidents and premiers at the height of the Cold War. We have seen the foundation of nations. We have seen the ringleaders of revolution. We have beheld saints who inspired us with hope, rebels who stirred us with passion, and heroes who emboldened us with courage — all here to share plans, proposals, visions, and ideas on the world's biggest stage.

Like those who met us before, our time is one of great contests, high stakes, and clear choices. The essential divide that runs all around the world and throughout history is once again thrown into stark relief. It is the divide between those whose thirst for control deludes them into thinking they are destined to rule over others and those people and nations who want only to rule themselves.

I have the immense privilege of addressing you today as the elected leader of a nation that prizes liberty, independence, and self-government above all. The United States, after having spent over two and a half trillion dollars since my election to completely rebuild our great military, is also, by far, the world's most powerful nation. Hopefully, it will never have to use this power.

Americans know that in a world where others seek conquest and domination, our nation must be strong in wealth, in might, and in spirit. That is why the United States vigorously defends the traditions and customs that have made us who we are.

Like my beloved country, each nation represented in this hall has a cherished history, culture, and heritage that is worth defending and celebrating, and which gives us our singular potential and strength.

The free world must embrace its national foundations. It must not attempt to erase them or replace them.

Looking around and all over this large, magnificent planet, the truth is plain to see: If you want freedom, take pride in your country. If you want democracy, hold on to your sovereignty. And if you want peace, love your nation. Wise leaders always put the good of their own people and their own country first.

The future does not belong to globalists. The future belongs to patriots. The future belongs to sovereign and independent nations who protect their citizens, respect their neighbors, and honor the differences that make each country special and unique.

It is why we in the United States have embarked on an exciting program of national renewal. In everything we do, we are focused on empowering the dreams and aspirations of our citizens.

Thanks to our pro-growth economic policies, our domestic unemployment rate reached its lowest level in over half a century. Fueled by massive tax cuts and regulations cuts, jobs are being produced at a historic rate. Six million Americans have been added to the employment rolls in under three years.

Last month, African American, Hispanic American, and Asian American unemployment reached their lowest rates ever recorded. We are marshaling our nation's vast energy abundance, and the United States is now the number one producer of oil and natural gas anywhere in the world. Wages are rising, incomes are soaring, and 2.5 million Americans have been lifted out of poverty in less than three years.

As we rebuild the unrivaled might of the American military, we are also revitalizing our alliances by making it very clear that all of our partners are expected to pay their fair share of the tremendous defense burden, which the United States has borne in the past.

At the center of our vision for national renewal is an ambitious campaign to reform international trade. For decades, the international trading system has been easily exploited by nations acting in very bad faith. As jobs were outsourced, a small handful grew wealthy at the expense of the middle class.

In America, the result was 4.2 million lost manufacturing jobs and $15 trillion in trade deficits over the last quarter century. The United States is now taking that decisive action to end this grave economic injustice. Our goal is simple: We want balanced trade that is both fair and reciprocal.

We have worked closely with our partners in Mexico and Canada to replace NAFTA with the brand new and hopefully bipartisan U.S.-Mexico-Canada Agreement.

Tomorrow, I will join Prime Minister Abe of Japan to continue our progress in finalizing a terrific new trade deal.

As the United Kingdom makes preparations to exit the European Union, I have made clear that we stand ready to complete an exceptional new trade agreement with the UK that will bring tremendous benefits to both of our countries. We are working closely with Prime Minister Boris Johnson on a magnificent new trade deal.

The most important difference in America's new approach on trade concerns our relationship with China. In 2001, China was admitted to the World Trade Organization. Our leaders then argued that this decision would compel China to liberalize its economy and strengthen protections to provide things that were unacceptable to us, and for private property and for the rule of law. Two decades later, this theory has been tested and proven completely wrong.

Not only has China declined to adopt promised reforms, it has embraced an economic model dependent on massive market barriers, heavy state subsidies, currency manipulation, product dumping, forced technology transfers, and the theft of intellectual property and also trade secrets on a grand scale.

As just one example, I recently met the CEO of a terrific American company, Micron Technology, at the White House. Micron produces memory chips used in countless electronics. To advance the Chinese government's five-year economic plan, a company owned by the Chinese state allegedly stole Micron's designs, valued at up to $8.7 billion. Soon, the Chinese company obtains patents for nearly an identical product, and Micron was banned from selling its own goods in China. But we are seeking justice.

The United States lost 60,000 factories after China entered the WTO. This is happening to other countries all over the globe.

The World Trade Organization needs drastic change. The second-largest economy in the world should not be permitted to declare itself a "developing country" in order to game the system at others' expense.

For years, these abuses were tolerated, ignored, or even encouraged. Globalism exerted a religious pull over past leaders, causing them to ignore their own national interests.

But as far as America is concerned, those days are over. To confront these unfair practices, I placed massive tariffs on more than $500 billion worth of Chinese-made goods. Already, as a result of these tariffs, supply chains are relocating back to America and to other nations, and billions of dollars are being paid to our Treasury.

The American people are absolutely committed to restoring balance to our relationship with China. Hopefully, we can reach an agreement that would be beneficial for both countries. But as I have made very clear, I will not accept a bad deal for the American people.

As we endeavor to stabilize our relationship, we're also carefully monitoring the situation in Hong Kong. The world fully expects that the Chinese government will honor its binding treaty, made with the British and registered with the United Nations, in which China commits to protect Hong Kong's freedom, legal system, and democratic ways of life. How China chooses to handle the situation will say a great deal about its role in the world in the future. We are all counting on President Xi as a great leader.

The United States does not seek conflict with any other nation. We desire peace, cooperation, and mutual gain with all. But I will never fail to defend America's interests.

One of the greatest security threats facing peace-loving nations today is the repressive regime in Iran. The regime's record of death and destruction is well known to us all. Not only is Iran the world's number one state sponsor of terrorism, but Iran's leaders are fueling the tragic wars in both Syria and Yemen.

At the same time, the regime is squandering the nation's wealth and future in a fanatical quest for nuclear weapons and the means to deliver them. We must never allow this to happen.

To stop Iran's path to nuclear weapons and missiles, I withdrew the United States from the terrible Iran nuclear deal, which has very little time remaining, did not allow inspection of important sites, and did not cover ballistic missiles.

Following our withdrawal, we have implemented severe economic sanctions on the country. Hoping to free itself from sanctions, the regime has escalated its violent and unprovoked aggression. In response to Iran's recent attack on Saudi Arabian oil facilities, we just imposed the highest level of sanctions on Iran's central bank and sovereign wealth fund.

All nations have a duty to act. No responsible government should subsidize Iran's bloodlust. As long as Iran's menacing behavior continues, sanctions will not be lifted; they will be tightened. Iran's leaders will have turned a proud nation into just another cautionary tale of what happens when a ruling class abandons its people and embarks on a crusade for personal power and riches.

For 40 years, the world has listened to Iran's rulers as they lash out at everyone else for the problems they alone have created. They conduct ritual chants of "Death to America" and traffic in monstrous anti-Semitism. Last year the country's Supreme Leader stated, "Israel is a malignant cancerous tumor…that has to be removed and eradicated: it is possible and it will happen." America will never tolerate such anti-Semitic hate.

Fanatics have long used hatred of Israel to distract from their own failures. Thankfully, there is a growing recognition in the wider Middle East that the countries of the region share common interests in battling extremism and unleashing economic opportunity. That is why it is so important to have full, normalized relations between Israel and its neighbors. Only a relationship built on common interests, mutual respect, and religious tolerance can forge a better future.

Iran's citizens deserve a government that cares about reducing poverty, ending corruption, and increasing jobs — not stealing their money to fund a massacre abroad and at home.

After four decades of failure, it is time for Iran's leaders to step forward and to stop threatening other countries, and focus on building up their own country. It is time for Iran's leaders to finally put the Iranian people first.

America is ready to embrace friendship with all who genuinely seek peace and respect.

Many of America's closest friends today were once our gravest foes. The United States has never believed in permanent enemies. We want partners, not adversaries. America knows that while anyone can make war, only the most courageous can choose peace.

For this same reason, we have pursued bold diplomacy on the Korean Peninsula. I have told Kim Jong Un what I truly believe: that, like Iran, his country is full of tremendous untapped potential, but that to realize that promise, North Korea must denuclearize.

Around the world, our message is clear: America's goal is lasting, America's goal is harmony, and America's goal is not to go with these endless wars — wars that never end.

With that goal in mind, my administration is also pursuing the hope of a brighter future in Afghanistan. Unfortunately, the Taliban has chosen to continue their savage attacks. And we will continue to work with our coalition of Afghan partners to stamp out terrorism, and we will never stop working to make peace a reality.

Here in the Western Hemisphere, we are joining with our partners to ensure stability and opportunity all across the region. In that mission, one of our most critical challenges is illegal immigration, which undermines prosperity, rips apart societies, and empowers ruthless criminal cartels.

Mass illegal migration is unfair, unsafe, and unsustainable for everyone involved: the sending countries and the depleted countries. And they become depleted very fast, but their youth is not taken care of and human capital goes to waste.

The receiving countries are overburdened with more migrants than they can responsibly accept. And the migrants themselves are exploited, assaulted, and abused by vicious coyotes. Nearly one third of women who make the journey north to our border are sexually assaulted along the way. Yet, here in the United States and around the world, there is a growing cottage industry of radical activists and non-governmental organizations that promote human smuggling. These groups encourage illegal migration and demand erasure of national borders.

Today, I have a message for those open border activists who cloak themselves in the rhetoric of social justice: Your policies are not just. Your policies are cruel and evil. You are empowering criminal organizations that prey on innocent men, women, and children. You put your own false sense of virtue before the lives, wellbeing, and [of] countless innocent people. When you undermine border security, you are undermining human rights and human dignity.

Many of the countries here today are coping with the challenges of uncontrolled migration. Each of you has the absolute right to protect your borders, and so, of course, does our country. Today, we must resolve to work together to end human smuggling, end human trafficking, and put these criminal networks out of business for good.

To our country, I can tell you sincerely: We are working closely with our friends in the region — including Mexico, Canada, Guatemala, Honduras, El Salvador, and Panama — to uphold the integrity of borders and ensure safety and prosperity for our people. I would like to thank President López Obrador of Mexico for the great cooperation we are receiving and for right now putting 27,000 troops on our southern border. Mexico is showing us great respect, and I respect them in return.

The U.S., we have taken very unprecedented action to stop the flow of illegal immigration. To anyone considering crossings of our border illegally, please hear these words: Do not pay the smugglers. Do not pay the coyotes. Do not put yourself in danger. Do not put your children in danger. Because if you make it here, you will not be allowed in; you will be promptly returned home. You will not be released into our country. As long as I am President of the United States, we will enforce our laws and protect our borders.

For all of the countries of the Western Hemisphere, our goal is to help people invest in the bright futures of their own nation. Our region is full of such incredible promise: dreams waiting to be built and national destinies for all. And they are waiting also to be pursued.

Throughout the hemisphere, there are millions of hardworking, patriotic young people eager to build, innovate, and achieve. But these nations cannot reach their potential if a generation of youth abandon their homes in search of a life elsewhere. We want every nation in our region to flourish and its people to thrive in freedom and peace.

In that mission, we are also committed to supporting those people in the Western Hemisphere who live under brutal oppression, such as those in Cuba, Nicaragua, and Venezuela.

According to a recent report from the U.N. Human Rights Council, women in Venezuela stand in line for 10 hours a day waiting for food. Over 15,000 people have been detained as political prisoners. Modern-day death squads are carrying out thousands of extrajudicial killings.

The dictator Maduro is a Cuban puppet, protected by Cuban bodyguards, hiding from his own people while Cuba plunders Venezuela's oil wealth to sustain its own corrupt communist rule.

Since I last spoke in this hall, the United States and our partners have built a historic coalition of 55 countries that recognize the legitimate government of Venezuela.

To the Venezuelans trapped in this nightmare: Please know that all of America is united behind you. The United States has vast quantities of humanitarian aid ready and waiting to be delivered. We are watching the Venezuela situation very closely. We await the day when democracy will be restored, when Venezuela will be free, and when liberty will prevail throughout this hemisphere.

One of the most serious challenges our countries face is the specter of socialism. It's the wrecker of nations and destroyer of societies.

Events in Venezuela remind us all that socialism and communism are not about justice, they are not about equality, they are not about lifting up the poor, and they are certainly not about the good of the nation. Socialism and communism are about one thing only: power for the ruling class.

Today, I repeat a message for the world that I have delivered at home: America will never be a socialist country.

In the last century, socialism and communism killed 100 million people. Sadly, as we see in Venezuela, the death toll continues in this country. These totalitarian ideologies, combined with modern technology, have the power to ~~excise~~ [exercise] new and disturbing forms of suppression and domination.

For this reason, the United States is taking steps to better screen foreign technology and investments and to protect our data and our security. We urge every nation present to do the same.

Freedom and democracy must be constantly guarded and protected, both abroad and from within. We must always be skeptical of those who want conformity and control. Even in free nations, we see alarming signs and new challenges to liberty.

A small number of social media platforms are acquiring immense power over what we can see and over what we are allowed to say. A permanent political class is openly disdainful, dismissive, and defiant of the will of the people. A faceless bureaucracy operates in secret and weakens democratic rule. Media and academic institutions push flat-out assaults on our histories, traditions, and values.

In the United States, my administration has made clear to social media companies that we will uphold the right of free speech. A free society cannot allow social media giants to silence the voices of the people, and a free people must never, ever be enlisted in the cause of silencing, coercing, canceling, or blacklisting their own neighbors.

As we defend American values, we affirm the right of all people to live in dignity. For this reason, my administration is working with other nations to stop criminalizing of homosexuality, and we stand in solidarity with LGBTQ people who live in countries that punish, jail, or execute individuals based upon sexual orientation.

We are also championing the role of women in our societies. Nations that empower women are much wealthier, safer, and much more politically stable. It is therefore vital not only to a nation's prosperity, but also is vital to its national security, to pursue women's economic development.

Guided by these principles, my administration launched the Women's Global Development and Prosperity Initiatives. The W-GDP is first-ever government-wide approach to women's economic empowerment, working to ensure that women all over the planet have the legal right to own and inherit property, work in the same industries as men, travel freely, and access credit and institutions.

Yesterday, I was also pleased to host leaders for a discussion about an ironclad American commitment: protecting religious leaders and also protecting religious freedom. This fundamental right is under growing threat around the world. Hard to believe, but 80 percent of the world's population lives in countries where religious liberty is in significant danger or even completely outlawed. Americans will never ~~fire or~~ tire in our effort to defend and promote freedom of worship and religion. We want and support religious liberty for all.

Americans will also never tire of defending innocent life. We are aware that many United Nations projects have attempted to assert a global right to taxpayer-funded abortion on demand, right up until the moment of delivery. Global bureaucrats have absolutely no business attacking the sovereignty of nations that wish to protect innocent life. Like many nations here today, we in America believe that every child — born and unborn — is a sacred gift from God.

There is no circumstance under which the United States will allow international ~~entries~~ [entities] to trample on the rights of our citizens, including the right to self-defense. That is why, this year, I announced that we will never ratify the U.N. Arms Trade Treaty, which would threaten the liberties of law-abiding American citizens. The United States will always uphold our constitutional right to keep and bear arms. We will always uphold our Second Amendment.

The core rights and values America defends today were inscribed in America's founding documents. Our nation's Founders understood that there will always be those who believe they are entitled to wield power and control over others. Tyranny advances under many names and many theories, but it always comes down to the desire for domination. It protects not the interests of many, but the privilege of few.

Our Founders gave us a system designed to restrain this dangerous impulse. They chose to entrust American power to those most invested in the fate of our nation: a proud and fiercely independent people.

The true good of a nation can only be pursued by those who love it: by citizens who are rooted in its history, who are nourished by its culture, committed to its values, attached to its people, and who know that its future is theirs to build or theirs to lose. Patriots see a nation and its destiny in ways no one else can.

Liberty is only preserved, sovereignty is only secured, democracy is only sustained, greatness is only realized, by the will and devotion of patriots. In their spirit is found the strength to resist oppression, the inspiration to forge legacy, the goodwill to seek friendship, and the bravery to reach for peace. Love of our nations makes the world better for all nations.

So to all the leaders here today, join us in the most fulfilling mission a person could have, the most profound contribution anyone can make: Lift up your nations. Cherish your culture. Honor your histories. Treasure your citizens. Make your countries strong, and prosperous, and righteous. Honor the dignity of your people, and nothing will be outside of your reach.

When our nations are greater, the future will be brighter, our people will be happier, and our partnerships will be stronger.

With God's help, together we will cast off the enemies of liberty and overcome the oppressors of dignity. We will set new standards of living and reach new heights of human achievement. We will rediscover old truths, unravel old mysteries, and make thrilling new breakthroughs. And we will find more beautiful friendship and more harmony among nations than ever before.

My fellow leaders, the path to peace and progress, and freedom and justice, and a better world for all humanity, begins at home.

Thank you. God bless you. God bless the nations of the world. And God bless America. Thank you very much. (Applause.)

**Speech by President Trump at South Dakota's 2020 Mount Rushmore
Fireworks Celebration**
July 3, 2020
Keystone, South Dakota

THE PRESIDENT: Well, thank you very much. And Governor Noem, Secretary Bernhardt — very much appreciate it — members of Congress, distinguished guests, and a very special hello to South Dakota. (Applause.)

As we begin this Fourth of July weekend, the First Lady and I wish each and every one of you a very, very Happy Independence Day. Thank you. (Applause.)

Let us show our appreciation to the South Dakota Army and Air National Guard, and the U.S. Air Force for inspiring us with that magnificent display of American air power — (applause) –and of course, our gratitude, as always, to the legendary and very talented Blue Angels. Thank you very much. (Applause.)

Let us also send our deepest thanks to our wonderful veterans, law enforcement, first responders, and the doctors, nurses, and scientists working tirelessly to kill the virus. They're working hard. (Applause.) I want to thank them very, very much.

We're grateful as well to your state's Congressional delegation: Senators John Thune — John, thank you very much — (applause) — Senator Mike Rounds — (applause) — thank you, Mike — and Dusty Johnson, Congressman. Hi, Dusty. Thank you. (Applause.) And all others with us tonight from Congress, thank you very much for coming. We appreciate it.

There could be no better place to celebrate America's independence than beneath this magnificent, incredible, majestic mountain and monument to the greatest Americans who have ever lived.

Today, we pay tribute to the exceptional lives and extraordinary legacies of George Washington, Thomas Jefferson, Abraham Lincoln, and Teddy Roosevelt. (Applause.) I am here as your President to proclaim before the country and before the world: This monument will never be desecrated — (applause) — these heroes will never be defaced, their legacy will never, ever be destroyed, their achievements will never be forgotten, and Mount Rushmore will stand forever as an eternal tribute to our forefathers and to our freedom. (Applause.)

AUDIENCE: USA! USA! USA!

THE PRESIDENT: We gather tonight to herald the most important day in the history of nations: July 4th, 1776. At those words, every American heart should swell with pride. Every American family should cheer with delight. And every American patriot should be filled with joy, because each of you lives in the most magnificent country in the history of the world, and it will soon be greater than ever before. (Applause.)

Our Founders launched not only a revolution in government, but a revolution in the pursuit of justice, equality, liberty, and prosperity. No nation has done more to advance the human condition than the United States of America. And no people have done more to promote human progress than the citizens of our great nation. (Applause.)

It was all made possible by the courage of 56 patriots who gathered in Philadelphia 244 years ago and signed the Declaration of Independence. (Applause.) They enshrined a divine truth that changed the world forever when they said: "...all men are created equal."

These immortal words set in motion the unstoppable march of freedom. Our Founders boldly declared that we are all endowed with the same divine rights — given [to] us by our Creator in Heaven. And that which God has given us, we will allow no one, ever, to take away — ever. (Applause.)

Seventeen seventy-six represented the culmination of thousands of years of western civilization and the triumph not only of spirit, but of wisdom, philosophy, and reason.

And yet, as we meet here tonight, there is a growing danger that threatens every blessing our ancestors fought so hard for, struggled, they bled to secure.

Our nation is witnessing a merciless campaign to wipe out our history, defame our heroes, erase our values, and indoctrinate our children.

AUDIENCE: Booo —

THE PRESIDENT: Angry mobs are trying to tear down statues of our Founders, deface our most sacred memorials, and unleash a wave of violent crime in our cities. Many of these people have no idea why they are doing this, but some know exactly what they are doing. They think the American people are weak and soft and submissive. But no, the American people are strong and proud, and they will not allow our country, and all of its values, history, and culture, to be taken from them. (Applause.)

AUDIENCE: USA! USA! USA!

THE PRESIDENT: One of their political weapons is "Cancel Culture" — driving people from their jobs, shaming dissenters, and demanding total submission from anyone who disagrees. This is the very definition of totalitarianism, and it is completely alien to our culture and our values, and it has absolutely no place in the United States of America. (Applause.) This attack on our liberty, our magnificent liberty, must be stopped, and it will be stopped very quickly. We will expose this dangerous movement, protect our nation's children, end this radical assault, and preserve our beloved American way of life. (Applause.)

In our schools, our newsrooms, even our corporate boardrooms, there is a new far-left fascism that demands absolute allegiance. If you do not speak its language, perform its rituals, recite its mantras, and follow its commandments, then you will be censored, banished, blacklisted, persecuted, and punished. It's not going to happen to us. (Applause.)

Make no mistake: this left-wing cultural revolution is designed to overthrow the American Revolution. In so doing, they would destroy the very civilization that rescued billions from poverty, disease, violence, and hunger, and that lifted humanity to new heights of achievement, discovery, and progress.

To make this possible, they are determined to tear down every statue, symbol, and memory of our national heritage.

AUDIENCE MEMBER: Not on my watch! (Applause.)

THE PRESIDENT: True. That's very true, actually. (Laughter.) That is why I am deploying federal law enforcement to protect our monuments, arrest the rioters, and prosecute offenders to the fullest extent of the law. (Applause.)

AUDIENCE: Four more years! Four more years! Four more years!

THE PRESIDENT: I am pleased to report that yesterday, federal agents arrested the suspected ringleader of the attack on the statue of Andrew Jackson in Washington, D.C. — (applause) — and, in addition, hundreds more have been arrested. (Applause.)

Under the executive order I signed last week — pertaining to the Veterans' Memorial Preservation and Recognition Act and other laws — people who damage or deface federal statues or monuments will get a minimum of 10 years in prison. (Applause.) And obviously, that includes our beautiful Mount Rushmore. (Applause.)

Our people have a great memory. They will never forget the destruction of statues and monuments to George Washington, Abraham Lincoln, Ulysses S. Grant, abolitionists, and many others.

The violent mayhem we have seen in the streets of cities that are run by liberal Democrats, in every case, is the predictable result of years of extreme indoctrination and bias in education, journalism, and other cultural institutions.

Against every law of society and nature, our children are taught in school to hate their own country, and to believe that the men and women who built it were not heroes, but that were villains. The radical view of American history is a web of lies — all perspective is removed, every virtue is obscured, every motive is twisted, every fact is distorted, and every flaw is magnified until the history is purged and the record is disfigured beyond all recognition.

This movement is openly attacking the legacies of every person on Mount Rushmore. They defile the memory of Washington, Jefferson, Lincoln, and Roosevelt. Today, we will set history and history's record straight. (Applause.)

133

Before these figures were immortalized in stone, they were American giants in full flesh and blood, gallant men whose intrepid deeds unleashed the greatest leap of human advancement the world has ever known. Tonight, I will tell you and, most importantly, the youth of our nation, the true stories of these great, great men.

From head to toe, George Washington represented the strength, grace, and dignity of the American people. From a small volunteer force of citizen farmers, he created the Continental Army out of nothing and rallied them to stand against the most powerful military on Earth.

Through eight long years, through the brutal winter at Valley Forge, through setback after setback on the field of battle, he led those patriots to ultimate triumph. When the Army had dwindled to a few thousand men at Christmas of 1776, when defeat seemed absolutely certain, he took what remained of his forces on a daring nighttime crossing of the Delaware River.

They marched through nine miles of frigid darkness, many without boots on their feet, leaving a trail of blood in the snow. In the morning, they seized victory at Trenton. After forcing the surrender of the most powerful empire on the planet at Yorktown, General Washington did not claim power, but simply returned to Mount Vernon as a private citizen.

When called upon again, he presided over the Constitutional Convention in Philadelphia, and was unanimously elected our first President. (Applause.) When he stepped down after two terms, his former adversary King George called him "the greatest man of the age." He remains first in our hearts to this day. For as long as Americans love this land, we will honor and cherish the father of our country, George Washington. (Applause.) He will never be removed, abolished, and most of all, he will never be forgotten. (Applause.)

Thomas Jefferson — the great Thomas Jefferson — was 33 years old when he traveled north to Pennsylvania and brilliantly authored one of the greatest treasures of human history, the Declaration of Independence. He also drafted Virginia's constitution, and conceived and wrote the Virginia Statute for Religious Freedom, a model for our cherished First Amendment.

After serving as the first Secretary of State, and then Vice President, he was elected to the Presidency. He ordered American warriors to crush the Barbary pirates, he doubled the size of our nation with the Louisiana Purchase, and he sent the famous explorers Lewis and Clark into the west on a daring expedition to the Pacific Ocean.

He was an architect, an inventor, a diplomat, a scholar, the founder of one of the world's great universities, and an ardent defender of liberty. Americans will forever admire the author of American freedom, Thomas Jefferson. (Applause.) And he, too, will never, ever be abandoned by us. (Applause.)

Abraham Lincoln, the savior of our union, was a self-taught country lawyer who grew up in a log cabin on the American frontier.

The first Republican President, he rose to high office from obscurity, based on a force and clarity of his anti-slavery convictions. Very, very strong convictions.

He signed the law that built the Transcontinental Railroad; he signed the Homestead Act, given to some incredible scholars — as simply defined, ordinary citizens free land to settle anywhere in the American West; and he led the country through the darkest hours of American history, giving every ounce of strength that he had to ensure that government of the people, by the people, and for the people did not perish from this Earth. (Applause.)

He served as Commander-in-Chief of the U.S. Armed Forces during our bloodiest war, the struggle that saved our union and extinguished the evil of slavery. Over 600,000 died in that war; more than 20,000 were killed or wounded in a single day at Antietam. At Gettysburg, 157 years ago, the Union bravely withstood an assault of nearly 15,000 men and threw back Pickett's charge.

Lincoln won the Civil War; he issued the Emancipation Proclamation; he led the passage of the 13th Amendment, abolishing slavery for all time — (applause) — and ultimately, his determination to preserve our nation and our union cost him his life. For as long as we live, Americans will uphold and revere the immortal memory of President Abraham Lincoln. (Applause.)

Theodore Roosevelt exemplified the unbridled confidence of our national culture and identity. He saw the towering grandeur of America's mission in the world and he pursued it with overwhelming energy and zeal.

As a Lieutenant Colonel during the Spanish-American War, he led the famous Rough Riders to defeat the enemy at San Juan Hill. He cleaned up corruption as Police Commissioner of New York City, then served as the Governor of New York, Vice President, and at 42 years old, became the youngest-ever President of the United States. (Applause.)

He sent our great new naval fleet around the globe to announce America's arrival as a world power. He gave us many of our national parks, including the Grand Canyon; he oversaw the construction of the awe-inspiring Panama Canal; and he is the only person ever awarded both the Nobel Peace Prize and the Congressional Medal of Honor. He was — (applause) — American freedom personified in full. The American people will never relinquish the bold, beautiful, and untamed spirit of Theodore Roosevelt. (Applause.)

No movement that seeks to dismantle these treasured American legacies can possibly have a love of America at its heart. Can't have it. No person who remains quiet at the destruction of this resplendent heritage can possibly lead us to a better future.

The radical ideology attacking our country advances under the banner of social justice. But in truth, it would demolish both justice and society. It would transform justice into an instrument of division and vengeance, and it would turn our free and inclusive society into a place of repression, domination, and exclusion.

They want to silence us, but we will not be silenced. (Applause.)

AUDIENCE: USA! USA! USA!

AUDIENCE MEMBER: We love you!

THE PRESIDENT: Thank you. Thank you very much. Thank you very much.

We will state the truth in full, without apology: We declare that the United States of America is the most just and exceptional nation ever to exist on Earth.

We are proud of the fact — (applause) — that our country was founded on Judeo-Christian principles, and we understand — (applause) — that these values have dramatically advanced the cause of peace and justice throughout the world.

We know that the American family is the bedrock of American life. (Applause.)

We recognize the solemn right and moral duty of every nation to secure its borders. (Applause.) And we are building the wall. (Applause.)

We remember that governments exist to protect the safety and happiness of their own people. A nation must care for its own citizens first. We must take care of America first. It's time. (Applause.)

We believe in equal opportunity, equal justice, and equal treatment for citizens of every race, background, religion, and creed. Every child, of every color — born and unborn — is made in the holy image of God. (Applause.)

We want free and open debate, not speech codes and cancel culture.

We embrace tolerance, not prejudice.

We support the courageous men and women of law enforcement. (Applause.) We will never abolish our police or our great Second Amendment, which gives us the right to keep and bear arms. (Applause.)

We believe that our children should be taught to love their country, honor our history, and respect our great American flag. (Applause.)

We stand tall, we stand proud, and we only kneel to Almighty God. (Applause.)

This is who we are. This is what we believe. And these are the values that will guide us as we strive to build an even better and greater future.

Those who seek to erase our heritage want Americans to forget our pride and our great dignity, so that we can no longer understand ourselves or America's destiny. In toppling the heroes of 1776, they seek to dissolve the bonds of love and loyalty that we feel for our country, and that we feel for each other. Their goal is not a better America, their goal is the end of America.

AUDIENCE: Booo —

THE PRESIDENT: In its place, they want power for themselves. But just as patriots did in centuries past, the American people will stand in their way — and we will win, and win quickly and with great dignity. (Applause.)

We will never let them rip America's heroes from our monuments, or from our hearts. By tearing down Washington and Jefferson, these radicals would tear down the very heritage for which men gave their lives to win the Civil War; they would erase the memory that inspired those soldiers to go to their deaths, singing these words of the Battle Hymn of the Republic: "As He died to make men Holy, let us die to make men free, while God is marching on." (Applause.)

They would tear down the principles that propelled the abolition of slavery in America and, ultimately, around the world, ending an evil institution that had plagued humanity for thousands and thousands of years. Our opponents would tear apart the very documents that Martin Luther King used to express his dream, and the ideas that were the foundation of the righteous movement for Civil Rights. They would tear down the beliefs, culture, and identity that have made America the most vibrant and tolerant society in the history of the Earth.

My fellow Americans, it is time to speak up loudly and strongly and powerfully and defend the integrity of our country. (Applause.)

AUDIENCE: USA! USA! USA!

THE PRESIDENT: It is time for our politicians to summon the bravery and determination of our American ancestors. It is time. (Applause.) It is time to plant our flag and protect the greatest of this nation, for citizens of every race, in every city, and every part of this glorious land. For the sake of our honor, for the sake of our children, for the sake of our union, we must protect and preserve our history, our heritage, and our great heroes. (Applause.)

Here tonight, before the eyes of our forefathers, Americans declare again, as we did 244 years ago: that we will not be tyrannized, we will not be demeaned, and we will not be intimidated by bad, evil people. It will not happen. (Applause.)

AUDIENCE: USA! USA! USA!

THE PRESIDENT: We will proclaim the ideals of the Declaration of Independence, and we will never surrender the spirit and the courage and the cause of July 4th, 1776.

Upon this ground, we will stand firm and unwavering. In the face of lies meant to divide us, demoralize us, and diminish us, we will show that the story of America unites us, inspires us, includes us all, and makes everyone free.

We must demand that our children are taught once again to see America as did Reverend Martin Luther King, when he said that the Founders had signed "a promissory note" to every future generation. Dr. King saw that the mission of justice required us to fully embrace our founding ideals. Those ideals are so important to us — the founding ideals. He called on his fellow citizens not to rip down their heritage, but to live up to their heritage. (Applause.)

Above all, our children, from every community, must be taught that to be American is to inherit the spirit of the most adventurous and confident people ever to walk the face of the Earth.

Americans are the people who pursued our Manifest Destiny across the ocean, into the uncharted wilderness, over the tallest mountains, and then into the skies and even into the stars.

We are the country of Andrew Jackson, Ulysses S. Grant, and Frederick Douglass. We are the land of Wild Bill Hickock and Buffalo Bill Cody. (Applause.) We are the nation that gave rise to the Wright Brothers, the Tuskegee Airmen — (applause) — Harriet Tubman, Clara Barton, Jesse Owens, George Patton — General George Patton — the great Louie Armstrong, Alan Shepard, Elvis Presley, and Mohammad Ali. (Applause.) And only America could have produced them all. (Applause.) No other place.

We are the culture that put up the Hoover Dam, laid down the highways, and sculpted the skyline of Manhattan. We are the people who dreamed a spectacular dream — it was called: Las Vegas, in the Nevada desert; who built up Miami from the Florida marsh; and who carved our heroes into the face of Mount Rushmore. (Applause.)

Americans harnessed electricity, split the atom, and gave the world the telephone and the Internet. We settled the Wild West, won two World Wars, landed American astronauts on the Moon — and one day very soon, we will plant our flag on Mars.

We gave the world the poetry of Walt Whitman, the stories of Mark Twain, the songs of Irving Berlin, the voice of Ella Fitzgerald, the style of Frank Sinatra — (applause) — the comedy of Bob Hope, the power of the Saturn V rocket, the toughness of the Ford F-150 — (applause) — and the awesome might of the American aircraft carriers.

Americans must never lose sight of this miraculous story. You should never lose sight of it, because nobody has ever done it like we have done it. So today, under the authority vested in me as President of the United States — (applause) — I am announcing the creation of a new monument to the giants of our past. I am signing an executive order to establish the National Garden of American Heroes, a vast outdoor park that will feature the statues of the greatest Americans to ever live. (Applause.)

From this night and from this magnificent place, let us go forward united in our purpose and re-dedicated in our resolve. We will raise the next generation of American patriots. We will write the next thrilling chapter of the American adventure. And we will teach our children to know that they live in a land of legends, that nothing can stop them, and that no one can hold them down. (Applause.) They will know that in America, you can do anything, you can be anything, and together, we can achieve anything. (Applause.)

Uplifted by the titans of Mount Rushmore, we will find unity that no one expected; we will make strides that no one thought possible. This country will be everything that our citizens have hoped for, for so many years, and that our enemies fear — because we will never forget that American freedom exists for American greatness. And that's what we have: American greatness. (Applause.)

Centuries from now, our legacy will be the cities we built, the champions we forged, the good we did, and the monuments we created to inspire us all.

My fellow citizens: America's destiny is in our sights. America's heroes are embedded in our hearts. America's future is in our hands. And ladies and gentlemen: the best is yet to come. (Applause.)

AUDIENCE: USA! USA! USA!

THE PRESIDENT: This has been a great honor for the First Lady and myself to be with you. I love your state. I love this country. I'd like to wish everybody a very happy Fourth of July. To all, God bless you, God bless your families, God bless our great military, and God bless America. Thank you very much. (Applause.)

Afterword

If We Don't Act, 2% of the People
Are About to Control the Other 98%

By Lt. Gen. Michael T. Flynn (Ret.)

I was once told if we're not careful, 2 percent of the passionate will control 98 percent of the indifferent 100 percent of the time.

The more I've thought about this phrase, the more I believe it. There is now a small group of passionate people working hard to destroy our American way of life. Treason and treachery are rampant and our rule of law and those law enforcement professionals who uphold our laws are under the gun more than at any time in our nation's history. These passionate 2 percent appear to be winning.

Despite there being countless good people trying to come to grips with everything else on their plates, our silent majority (the indifferent) can no longer be silent.

If the United States wants to survive the onslaught of socialism, if we are to continue to enjoy self-government and the liberty of our hard-fought freedoms, we have to understand there are two opposing forces: One is the "children of light" and the other is the "children of darkness."

As I recently wrote, the art and exercise of self-governance require active participation by every American. I wasn't kidding! And voting is only part of that active participation. Time and again, the silent majority have been overwhelmed by the "audacity and resolve" of small, well-organized, passionate groups. It's now time for us, the silent majority (the indifferent), to demonstrate both.

The trials of our current times, like warfare, are immense and consequences severe and these seem inconquerable.

As a policewoman from Virginia told me, "People don't feel safe in their homes and our police force is so demoralized we cannot function as we should. In my 23 years with my department, I have never seen morale so low."

Another woman from Mississippi told me that we need our leaders to "drop a forceful hammer. People are losing patience. It simply must be stopped! Laws MUST be enforced … no one is above the law."

Don't fret. Through smart, positive actions of resolute citizen-patriots, we can prevail. Always keep in mind that our enemy (these dark forces) invariably have difficulties of which we are ignorant.

For most Americans, these forces appear to be strong. I sense they are desperate. I also sense that only a slight push on our part is all that is required to defeat these forces. How should that push come?

Prayers help and prayers matter, but action is also a remedy. Our law enforcement professionals, from the dispatcher to the detective and from the cop to the commissioner, are a line of defense against the corrupt and the criminal. It is how we remain (for now) in a state of relatively peaceful existence.

We must support them with all our being. They are not the enemy; they bring light to the darkness of night through their bravery and determination to do their jobs without fanfare and with tremendous sacrifice.

The silent majority (the indifferent) tend to go the way of those leading them. We are not map- or mind-readers; we are humans fraught with all the hopes and fears that flesh is heir to. We must not become lost in this battle. We must resoundingly follow our God-given common sense.

Seek the truth, fight for it in everything that is displayed before you. Don't trust the fake news or false prophets; trust your instincts and your common sense. Those with a conscience know the difference between right and wrong, and those with courage will always choose the harder right over the easier wrong.

I believe the attacks being presented to us today are part of a well-orchestrated and well-funded effort that uses racism as its sword to aggravate our battlefield dispositions. This weapon is used to leverage and legitimize violence and crime, not to seek or serve the truth.

The dark forces' weapons formed against us serve one purpose: to promote radical social change through power and control. Socialism and the creation of a socialist society are their ultimate goals.

They are also intent on driving God out of our families, our schools and our courts. They are even seeking the very removal of God from our churches, essentially hoping to remove God from our everyday lives.

Remember, we will only remain united as "one nation under God."

And yes, there is a "resistance movement" by the forces of darkness. However, we must also resist these onslaughts and instead take an optimistic view of our situation. Like war, optimism can be pervasive and helps to subdue any rising sense of fear.

We must, however, be deliberate about our optimism. Otherwise, we may get lost in discouragement and despair of any failings we encounter. We must be tenacious in the ultimate end we wish to gain. That end is to remain an unwavering constitutional republic based on a set of Judeo-Christian values and principles. We must not fear these and instead embrace each.

Our path requires course corrections. To move our experiment in democracy forward, we should fight and reject the tired and failed political paths and instead pursue a more correct path that shines a bright light on liberty, a path with greater and greater control of our livelihoods instead of being controlled by fewer and fewer of the too-long-in-power politicians. They have discarded us like old trash.

Our will, our individual liberties and freedoms, remain powerful forces and must be understood and applied smartly. We must not be overly stubborn. Following the Constitution as our guide and adapting to change as we have throughout history, we learn more about what freedoms humans desire.

At times, however, we have to fall back on what got us here. We cannot afford to lose our God-given human rights and the strong inner desire for freedom to choose and to breathe the fresh air of liberty. We must stand up and speak out to challenge our so-called "leaders" of government. We put them in charge; we can remove them as well.

It is through our rights and privileges as American citizens that we challenge the political class and leverage our election process so "we the people" can decide who will govern.

We must not allow a small percentage of the powerful to overtake our position on America's battlefield. We, as free-thinking and acting individuals, must control how we will live and not allow a few passionate others to change our way of life.

To the silent and currently indifferent majority: Wake up. America is at risk of being lost in the dustbin of history to socialism. The very heart and soul of America is at stake.

In war, as in life, most failure comes from inaction. We face a pivotal moment that can change the course of history of our nation.

We the people must challenge every politician at every level.

We also must stand and support our law enforcement professionals: They are the pointy end of the spear defending us against anarchy.

Now is the time to act.

About the Authors

Ed Martin is the hand-picked successor of Phyllis Schlafly to run her Eagle organizations and currently is President of the Phyllis Schlafly Eagles. He is co-author of the New York Times bestseller *The Conservative Case for Trump* (Regnery, 2016) and served as a Pro-Trump commentator on CNN and the host of the Salem Radio network's daily radio show Ed Martin's Pro America Report.

Ed was elected Chairman of the Missouri Republican Party in January 2013 and served on the Republican National Committee until 2015. In 2010, Ed was the Republican nominee for Congress coming within a few thousand votes of beating the incumbent Democrat in the historic Dick Gephardt district. In 2012, Ed was the Republican nomination for Missouri Attorney General while also serving as the Missouri Victor GOTV chairman.

Ed was chief of staff to Missouri Governor Matt Blunt from 2006-2008 helping Missouri leadership pass pro-life legislation, school choice laws, and limiting the reach of the left-wing government unions. In 2005, Ed was appointed Chairman of the St. Louis Board of Election Commissioners. He took the lead in taking on ACORN, stream-lined the office, and implemented the Help America Vote Act. In 2006, Ed was the McGivney Legal Fellow at Americans United for Life and served as lead counsel suing then-Governor Rod Blagojevich for Illinois' imposition on pro-life professionals.

Ed holds a law degree and advanced degrees in medical ethics and philosophy and was awarded post-graduate fellowships in Indonesia (Watson Fellowship) and Italy (Rotary Fellowship). After law school, Ed delayed a one year judicial clerkship to serve his church. As the director of the Human Rights Office for the church, Ed led the church community in educating and advocating for pro-life issues, educational opportunities for all, and outreach to the community as part of the new evangelization. It was during this time that Ed learned how Obama-esque "community organizing" was infiltrating our local community. Ed led a successful fight to defund the ACORN-affiliate Missouri Pro-Vote.

Ed spent the summer working at the Institute for Justice in Washington, D.C. assisting on the historic school choice Supreme Court case *Zelman v. Simmons-Harris*. During the 2001-02 term of the federal Court of Appeals for Eighth Circuit, Ed served a judicial clerk to Reagan-appointee Hon. Pasco M. Bowman, II. Immediately following his clerkship, he joined

146

the St. Louis-based international law firm Bryan Cave, LLC specializing in commercial litigation. In the fall of 2004, Ed left Bryan Cave and started his own law firm. He specialized in litigation and small business practice. He was President of the St. Louis Federalist Society and host for the historic Missouri visit of Associate Justice Antonin Scalia in 2004. He has served as executive director of Missouri Club for Growth and founded Missourians United for Life.

Ed and his wife Carol, a physician specializing in geriatric internal medicine, reside in Great Falls, Virginia with their four children.

***

Jordan Henry is the Director of Research for Phyllis Schlafly Eagles. He was hired to work full-time in 2017 after honing his writing skills under Phyllis Schlafly's direct editorial oversight for two summers. From 2015 until taking his present full-time position, he worked at Phyllis's request as a freelance contributing writer for her three-minute daily radio commentaries. In 2016, he was able to attend the Republican National Convention as an aide to Phyllis.

As the Director of Research, Jordan is responsible for promoting the conservative values Phyllis Schlafly championed for seven decades. He heads an ever-changing array of research projects studying Phyllis's life and works. He serves a lead role in coordinating events such as Phyllis Schlafly Eagles's annual Eagle Council. He also continues to write for the Phyllis Schlafly Report Radio Commentaries every month.

Jordan is a graduate of Pensacola Christian College. He and his wife Edith live in High Ridge, Missouri.

CPSIA information can be obtained
at www.ICGtesting.com
Printed in the USA
JSHW040148160920
7957JS00002B/4